THE POWER OF WATER

MW00682826

Waterobics and Water Fitness Exercises for All Ages

Ursula Pahlow

Sagamore Publishing Inc.
Champaign, IL 61824-0673

The publisher assumes no responsibility for any personal injury, property damage, or other loss suffered in activities related to the information presented in this book.

© 1991 Sagamore Publishing Co, Inc.
Champaign, IL, 61824-0673

All rights reserved. No part of this book may be reproduced in any form or by any means without permission in writing from the publisher.

Book design: Susan M. Williams
Cover design: Cindy Carlson
Illustrations: Taylor White
Photographs: Ursula Pahlow

Printed in the United States of America

Library of Congress Catalog Card Number:90-62328
ISBN:0-915611-26-0

I would like to dedicate this work to all individuals of any shape, age, and size who from now on will be exercising in water for their personal enjoyment and physical fitness.

The stress and agony of high and low impact exercise programs on land shall hereby be put aside forever to open all doors to the unique and wonderful way of exercising in water, learning to appreciate the power of water.

Contents

Acknowledgments

A sincere "thank you" to Eberhard, my husband, for his endless efforts to help with the completion of my work. He enthusiastically believes in exercising and fullheartedly supports my efforts of sharing my experience in water exercising. Without his involvement, none of this would have been possible.

I would like to thank my mother Kitty; my daughters, Heike and Crisanne; my son Oliver; my sister-in-law Renate, my brother Klaus; my granddaughters, Anne-Janyn and Melissa-Marie, my grandson Anthony, and my nephew Ansgar for their support.

To my most sincere friends, students, and colleagues, Alice, Alvada, Anne, Brenda, Bobbi, Bonnie, Cathy, Carol, Cheryl, Clara, Dave, Debbie, Donna, Eddie, George, Georgianna, Jacky, Jean, Joyce, Judy, John, Kathy, Ken, Kim, Lorraine, Mary, Matt, Maud, Nancy, Peggy, Sandy, Sharon, Terrie, Velva, Violet, and many more. . . you keep my adrenaline going! I sincerely enjoy guiding you through class and exercising with you since I need it just the same as you.

I would also like to thank Carol Taradejna for years of caring and devotion.

My appreciation goes to the Bolingbrook, Illinois Park District and to the Bolingbrook, Illinois Aquatic Center for their encouraging support.

And last but not least my sincere thanks to Susan Williams, Michelle Dressen, Lisa Braddock, Cindy Carlson, and the staff from Sagamore Publishing for their expertise and efforts in transforming my manuscript into a book. Thank you all.

Introduction

Aquatic exercises are becoming one of the most popular fitness activities in the United States. Even though swimming for recreation, fitness, or competition is nothing new, exercising in the water, taking advantage of water resistance, and making the most of water support will be the preferred way to exercise by the end of this century. Along with the water fitness craze, the demand for indoor swimming pools will greatly rise as well. How and why did this desire for frolicking and exercising in water come about? After all, we are not meant to be in water, anatomically speaking.

Looking back, it is now clear that exercising has gone through a natural evolution and progression, along with scientific discoveries and increased knowledge of physiology. Long-term exercising in the gym or health clubs, running, and competitive sports eventually created a variety of physical problems. Due to these occurring and recurring injuries, physicians began to recommend swimming to their patients rather than aerobics, jazzercise, or running. Low-impact aerobics seems to have gained in popularity, because it gives the exercisers a somewhat soothing feeling that they are physically active but at the same time they are still nursing their injuries.

Walking and speed walking became a substitute for runners with shin, ankle, or knee injuries. However, even though the air intake and the leg muscle exercise is good from fast walking, and even though the low-impact exercises are reaching muscles, the body weight is still bearing down on the hips, knees, and ankles. All the designer floors, shoes, fashions, and other gimmicks cannot prevent the wear and tear of body joints.

A lot of people had no choice but to turn to swimming for their physical fitness, and swimming lessons began to flourish nationwide. However, there was another water activity gaining popularity, known mostly to doctors, physical therapists, and their patients: water therapy.

Water therapy was designed to help improve and strengthen damaged body parts by using various techniques, while being surrounded by the soothing element of water. In water therapy, the body is being reintroduced to movement, with repetitious, slow, and deliberate exercises helping to mobilize stiffened joints and helping to tone muscles that have been neglected due to injury. Eventually the body responds in various degrees to this treatment.

In water, body movements became more and more sophisticated, the tempo of movement was adjusted, and different equipment was used to enhance the degree of water resistance. Music also became a popular background addition, because everyone was used to it from the days of aerobics. Somewhere along the line, instructors learned how to take advantage of different musical rhythms in the water as well. All this meant full advantage was taken of the water. Some instructors called their programs "aquarobics," "waterobics," "watercise" or "aqua/waterfit." People of all ages and both genders, as well as people with different physical abilities—including prenatal and postnatal conditions—began to work out in the water.

However, the ideas did not stop there. Swim instructors began to discover that the kickboard, for instance, could also be used to strengthen arm, abdomen, and back muscles. Hand paddles, fins and other aquatic accessories readily available around swimming pools began to receive more and more attention. Imagination opened doors to other water exercise creations all over the country.

Needless to say, we are now facing a nationwide study of all kinds of exercises and equipment used in water exercise activities. Studies include finding which methods are best, which equipment offers the most resistance, which combinations of movements are the most beneficial for the overall physical fitness workout, and which ones are safe to use for the individual exerciser.

Up to this date, no single water-related activity, method, or even routine has been proven the best or perfect way to be used at all times. Depending on certain factors such as personal preference, personal needs, the availability of equipment, and water and air temperature, the material used and the intensity and variety of exercises should be adjusted and changed from course to course. No one type of exercise routine should be applied over and over again if the program is to be efficient. The field is wide open.

A wide variety of ideas has surfaced in the past five to ten years. Physical fitness instructors, dance instructors, jazzercize and aerobic instructors, even karate, yoga, swimming, and basketball coaches got in on the action. Each thought they had found the ideal water workouts and wanted to share those with the nation.

Former aerobic instructors taking their studio routines to the water will soon discover that body movement in the water is very different from movement on land. Thus, the methods need to be adjusted. Basketball coaches, and yoga or dance instructors may all know some moves that are efficient in the water, but they (instructors) should certainly not insist on an entire class time using the traditional gym or studio routine.

Video productions on how to perform aerobic routines in water are becoming another form of relating ideas. However, those using land moves and routines that lead the public to believe that this is the way to exercise in water are incorrect. As a direct result of this misleading information, a whole chain of brand new water instructors across the nation are actually teaching the incorrect way to exercise in water. I feel it is time to inform the public and retrain water fitness instructors in revised moves and specific water exercises, including the use of equipment for best results in water.

Instructors have to ask themselves what it is they would like their students to accomplish. It is important to realize that movements in the water will be considerably slower than on deck. Therefore, perspiring instructors teaching from the pool side do not necessarily have perspiring pupils in the water. Fast rhythms for exercising on land do not necessarily work with the same moves in the water, especially if equipment is used to enhance water resistance. Standing or slowly moving in waist deep water for 30 minutes, keeping the upper torso exposed to the air and worrying about getting the hair wet, reflects an insufficient knowledge of water movement, and will lead clientele to believe that "water exercises don't do a thing for me."

xi

The slow warm-up period we are used to from the gym does not apply in the same sense to water warm up. Upon first entering the water, the body is warmer than the water. In fact, the warmer the air temperature, the colder the water seems to be. In that case, in order to avoid stiffening of the muscles, the body has to be moved moderately fast for at least 10-15 minutes, in some cases even longer to help adjust to the water and air temperature. However, in case of high air/water temperature, and in addition perhaps high humidity, the overall class tempo needs to be adjusted to a slower pace in order to avoid overexhaustion. At the end of the total workout, the body needs to be limbered and movements should slow down. It is a misconception that the exerciser has to be exhausted in order to have had a good workout. The same is true with heart rate. In the past, instructors (and as a result of their information, exercisers) thought the only way to have a good workout meant to have a high heart rate. On the contrary, 35-45 minutes of uninterrupted arm and leg movements in deep water, with (or better without) floating support will burn more calories and firm more muscles than a 15-20 minute jog/jump/leap period raising the heart rate to a maximum.

Heart rate elevation depends on a lot of things, including age, physical fitness status, health, body weight, air/water temperature, humidity, emotional status, extended breath holding, and most importantly the use of certain medications or even alcoholic beverages (which is definitely not recommended before or during exercising). The better the public is informed about the "hows" and "whys," the better the results may be.

This leads to the conclusion that more education on the power of in-water exercising, when and how to apply exercises and equipment, and most importantly, the knowledge of which movements in different instances are good for the body is called for. Water fitness instructors have to be very flexible in preparing their programs. They need to be able to adjust to any situation, depending on air-water temperature, humidity, and students' needs. The instructor has to be knowledgeable enough to change movements, equipment, or water depth to suit each situation.

All explanations about water-related exercises in this book are based on an eight-year study in waterobics as well as in water exercise programs with male and female students of all ages.

All exercises shown in this book are only suggestions that may be performed at a slow, moderate, or fast speed, according to the individual's personal needs and progression. Any combination of exercises from this book may be used based on class structure and fitness level of the class majority. Water exercising and waterobics will be very effective if performed sensibly and on a regular basis.

Weight loss is not the immediate goal upon starting a water exercise program—improving the overall physical condition should be the target. However, a doctor-approved dietary program along with a waterobics program is the ideal combination for eliminating excess weight and firming the body at the same time. Exercisers should keep in mind: "It is not what your body can do for you, it is what you should do for your body."

Ursula Pahlow
1991

The Power of Water

Exercising in water has existed for many years, and more and more doctors are recommending it. In fact, up to now it was most commonly used as a way to rehabilitate after a physical mishap that called for therapeutic treatment. It is still used in this way today. Another wonderful activity has evolved that is a combined extension of the therapeutic use of the power of the water, and the enjoyment of swimming: water exercising.

All movements in the water are supported, and at the same time resisted by the power of water. Movements are slowed down and elegantly executed. Bounces are cushioned by soft landings, and heavy bodies become nearly weightless in water. Hard-to-move body parts on land become miraculously agile in water. What better elements could be asked for?

The power of water helps to loosen stiffened joints, stretch tight muscles, and also firm soft muscles. It helps to tone and strengthen neglected bodies, and can even help to improve the cardiovascular system, while enhancing physical endurance. One of the best ways to achieve physical fitness is by using water power.

Depending on the individual's physical condition prior to exercising in water, movements can be fast or slow. All beginners in any type of exercise program must start out slowly. It is important to condition the body gradually, before graduating to faster, more vigorous movements.

With the development of water-related exercises, new terms such as "Waterobics" or "Aquarobics" were born. They are the counterparts of the land-related physical fitness programs known as "aerobics" and "low-impact aerobics." Waterobics replaces the stressful and many times damaging exercises done on land.

The entire body is absorbed in a constant firming and toning harmony while moving through water.

A difference in tempo and rhythm set to music, combined with a variety of movements and tools to enhance water exercising, make it much more exciting to mold one's body into a desired shape. The secret formula once a goal has been set is:

Commit yourself, use common sense, and be persistent.

Waterobics

What does "waterobics" mean? The basic principles of aerobics are transferred into water.

1. Musical rhythms are used for the speed of movements during exercising.
2. The heart rate is monitored before, during, and after exercising.
3. The successions of warming up, peaking, maintaining, tapering off, and cooling down are equally important in the water.

However, the choice of movements, the force of movements, and the speed of movements lead to a most decisive difference between land and water exercising. In water, we have a unique choice of exercising in shallow water with mostly body weight to work with, compared to moving in chest to shoulder depth, achieving almost total water support, and creating a wonderful weightlessness.

Choosing to use the body as the sole exercise equipment is the basic ingredient, expanding into a manifold of variations to increase water support as well as water resistance. In each case, the body reaction is different, as is the use of muscles.

Beginners and advanced exercisers benefit from the variety offered in waterobics since the level and speed of performance is adjusted according to the individual's needs. Additional equipment can be used to further enhance or reinforce water resistance as well as water support.

Some similarities between water exercising and fitness programs on land are:

• The same muscle firmness can be accomplished through waterobics as land aerobics.

• The same target heart rate can be reached in water.

• The same level of physical fitness can be accomplished by water exercising as by physical fitness programs in the gym, health, or fitness club.

However, some significant differences in water exercising include:

1. Stress on joints is minimized due to water support.
2. Muscles are firmed by means of water resistance.
3. Endurance and the cardiovascular system are strengthened with slow motion-like movements.
4. A target heart rate is reached almost effortlessly.
5. Being overweight, pregnant, or having medical problems has little or no impact while exercising in water.
6. Age is no barrier to exercising in water due to water support, which enables effortless movements.

Safety

How safe is a water exercise or a waterobics class? As with all physical fitness programs, it is very important that a doctor's approval be given *before* starting such a program. This is in the participant's own best interest. Not all programs are safe for all people all the time. To assume that a program in water is automatically considered safe for your body is a misconception.

Water is an excellent element to exercise in. It gives even the heaviest person support, if this person is in a water level covering at least 75 percent of the body. One can start to feel body buoyancy as soon as the water reaches the upper chest and shoulders when standing in an upright position. In this depth, walking becomes difficult due to buoyancy, and loss of balance may be the result.

The impact of jumping and hopping up and down is lessened due to water support. Therefore, the stress on joints such as hips, knees, ankles, and feet is much reduced. These same movements are also more tolerable to the back, due to the lower impact from water support.

People with arthritis, back problems, or other physical ailments find it easier to exercise in water than on land. However, there are some misconceptions. Most people tend to think that with the buoyancy created while exercising in water, all movements are safe. In reality, restrictions must be made to ensure the safety of participants.

Each person should use common sense while exercising, and know his or her limits. No one knows your body better than you do. The instructor offers exercise suggestions for you to use as you see fit. With the presence of back problems, the use of leg lifts, upper torso bends, forceful movements, and body twisting should be evaluated by a physician to avoid any complications.

Limitation of movements of the limbs is easiest to tolerate in water due to the additional support. With near weightlessness, many more exercises are possible in the water. Paralysis or immobility can be temporarily overcome by the use of a flotation device in water, if water support is insufficient.

Exercise machines to strengthen the body can certainly be replaced by taking advantage of water resistance. Perspiration is definitely possible while exercising in water. This depends on the water and air temperature, as well as the degree and tempo of the exercises themselves.

Increasing the heart rate by exercising in water is just as easily achieved as working out on land. But here again it is important to know just how far to go. A target heart rate should be evaluated *before* class and monitored *during* the fast-paced exercises, and immediately thereafter.

Water and air temperature, as well as humidity, play an important part when exercising in water. If water or air temperature is raised above 85° Fahrenheit, the stress on the cardiovascular system is greater. A slower class pace is then recommended. Lower water or air temperatures allow for faster movements for a longer period of time. High humidity places greater stress on the entire system, and raises body temperature and heart rate prematurely, even during slower activities in water.

In case of pregnancy, a new target heart rate must be evaluated by the physician. The speed of exercises may have to be reduced, and the heart rate will have to be kept lower than usual to protect the unborn child. However, restrictions of movements are not necessary as long as they feel comfortable, and the physician does not disapprove.

The use of exercise equipment in water can be very helpful in achieving physical fitness. However, the body reaction to movements made with such tools should be understood *before* they are used. For a safe water exercise or waterobics program, a skill outline and skill explanations are beneficial. This information can be used by the concerned student for evaluation by a physician in case of any physical restrictions. The class instructor should be informed by the student of any physical restrictions before each class. Strenuous exercises can then be changed and safer methods used. The results will be satisfying if exercising is done consistently at regular intervals.

Heart Rate as Fitness Guideline

Before, during, and after any kind of aerobic activity, the heart rate has to be monitored in order to keep track of the individual's response to the exercises.

The heart rate should always be counted before starting the exercises to show the individual's starting heart rate. This should be close to her or his own resting heart rate. As the exercise pace increases, so should the heart rate. After five to eight minutes of fast-paced work, the heart can already reach the target heart rate.

In waterobics, the average student may have a weight problem, back- or joint-related problems, elevated blood pressure, arthritis, may be pregnant, may be postpartum, is recovering from surgery, or may be a smoker with shortness of breath. A lot of these students are in waterobics due to a doctor's recommendation. They cannot follow an aerobic land-based program due to their physical conditions, and seek the moderation of waterobics, which is more tolerable for them.

With this in mind, a waterobics program should be designed differently than a land aerobic program. The fast-paced exercises in water, combined with humidity, chlorine odor, water, and air temperature should never be stressful to students in class. A five- to eight-minute fast-paced section should be followed by something less strenuous to allow students to catch their breaths. This more moderate pace can then be extended for up to thirty or more minutes with various activities, all of which should be presented in a smooth flow of exercises with few interruptions.

Let us not forget that in water, the entire body has to work hard throughout all the exercises in order to maintain a face-up body position and a steady balance. For instance, by simply treading water, the arms are moving constantly to counter-balance the leg movements. By setting this exercise to fast-paced music, while encouraging the students to follow the rhythm of the music, a target heart rate can easily be reached. This heart rate can be maintained for as long as the student wishes by simply working as hard as possible with all exercises following thereafter. The target heart rate should be taken immediately after the short cardiovascular section (fast-paced exercises, including hops, skips, jumps, and leaps. Take the heart rate again after the more moderately-paced exercises including jogging, treading, flutter kicking, and swimming).

At the end of a 45- or 60-minute workout, with a one- to two-minute cool-down period in the water, the heart rate should be taken again, and should then come close to the starting heart rate.

To determine one's personal target heart rate, the following formula may be used:

Deduct your age from 220   220
                                                    -
This is your maximum heart rate= _____
Multiply by 75%   x
Add resting heart rate+
This is your target heart rate =

Note: individuals taking medication for high blood pressure will have a slower target heart rate than most other individuals due to the heart rate -slowing action of the medication.

The maximum heart rate will be higher than the target heart rate upon first starting in an aerobic program, especially after leading a sedentary lifestyle. The highest heart rate may in some cases reach 200 counts per minute or more. This is above the maximum heart rate, and too high. After exercising on a regular basis twice or three times per week for at least two months, the heart rate will stabilize and will come closer to the target. If the heart rate still elevates to 200 counts per minute or above after a three- to four-week regular exercise period, a doctor should be consulted as a precautionary measure. If the heart rate does not recover to a near-starting heart rate at the end of class after the cooling-off period, and continues to be high for the next 15 or even 30 minutes after class, a doctor should definitely be consulted. The heart rate itself can be easily counted. Count for six seconds and multiply the figure by ten. For instance: if eight beats were counted within the six seconds, 80 heart beats per minute is the count.

The pulsation can be found:

- On the inside of the wrist (pulse) following the thumb down to the wrist, applying mild pressure with two fingers.

- On the side of the neck (carotid artery) following away from the Adam's apple to the first groove before the main neck muscle, applying mild pressure with two fingers (on one side only).

Resting and target heart rates vary widely, especially if heart rate-slowing medication is taken by the student. Generalized scales should not be used as heart rate guidelines unless they have been updated to new physical fitness knowledge and standards.

Even the personal target heart rate figure the individual has established by means of the above-mentioned formula will not always be the same when monitored in class. Different physical or emotional factors may interfere, elevating or lowering the heart rate aside from its norm. For instance, if a virus invades the body and puts the system in a defensive state, the heart rate will most likely be elevated. If an emotionally upsetting or unusually stressful day preceded the physical fitness activity, the body requires a longer slowing-down period that day, with relaxation and cleansing of the mind after the class. Our body gives us signals when to slow down, and when it is all right to be more aggressive. We have to learn to listen to our bodies to avoid overdoing things.

Cardiovascular Exercises

After a two- to three-minute warming-up period, a gradually increasing fast-paced exercise period should be offered. This is the cardiovascular part of the class. Arm and leg movements are equally involved in achieving a higher heart rate, preferably a target heart rate. Such a period can be prolonged in water for as long as ten to fifteen minutes, after which an average class may continue with five to fifteen minutes of a more moderately-paced exercise tempo.

We don't want to forget that most students in waterobics or any water exercise program are there because of some physical condition. This condition may be a health problem, a weight problem, or a desire to get back into shape gradually. Therefore, we are in no rush to overdo things. In waterobics as well as in water exercises, physical fitness is achieved slowly but steadily. After the warmup, the heart rate should increase slowly by more arm movements up, to the side, or forward. The legs get involved with an increase of steps and tempo, forward and back, up and down, or side to side. Jogging in the water, hopping, and leaping are all methods of achieving a target heart rate. Perspiration will be felt if the air and water temperatures are at a level of approximately 85° Fahrenheit or higher. However, at temperatures this high, caution should be taken to reduce the highest-paced cardiovascular section into a moderately-paced activity due to the risk of fatigue and overexertion. All students will still get enough of a workout even though the tempo has been somewhat reduced.

After a time period of 15 to 20 minutes, the heart rate should be monitored. A student does not need to wait for an announced heart rate check, and can check his or her own any time. The target heart rate should have been reached by now, and other parts of the body (leg, arm, stomach, back) need to be exercised next.

The focus should not only be on cardiovascular exercising in a water exercise or waterobics class; emphasis should also be placed on overall physical fitness. To achieve physical fitness, check your heart rate, weight, upper arm, upper thigh, waist and hip measurements regularly, control your eating habits, and exercise on a regular basis.

2

How the Exercises Affect the Body

Loss of Weight and Inches

Surveys show that a major weight reduction is not achieved in a short period of time by exercise alone. However, by starting an exercise program and a doctor-approved dietary program at the same time, a much greater weight loss is possible. Both must be maintained until the desired goal has been reached, and then continued indefinitely in order to preserve the accomplishment.

The continuous exerciser should take body measurements at the beginning and end of each six- or eight-week exercise period to establish his or her personal progress in loss of weight and inches, or gain of muscle and firmness. Presently established generalized scales should not be considered accurate for every individual. With less body fat and more muscle, the body weight might be higher than what generalized scales show. For instance, if you have been exercising on a regular basis, and you have reached your ideal clothes size, but your body weight is higher, the fatty tissue was burned off, and firmness and muscle took over. However, muscle is heavier in weight than fat. As the body begins to tone, a measurable reduction of inches can be recorded and clothes begin to feel more comfortable, soon to be replaced by a smaller size.

Lower Back and Water Exercises

Exercising in water can certainly strengthen the back if it is done with caution. Side bending as well as twisting or arching the back is not recommended in the case of lower back problems.

Holding on backwards to the wall may cause shoulder as well as upper back discomfort, and should be limited to a minimum of repetitions until the body has adjusted or is stronger. Since most exercises involve the lower back, it is recommended that the student learn to hold his stomach muscles contracted to help strengthen them. Firm stomach muscle support is the first step toward a healthier back.

Any water exercises involving laying on the stomach, arching the back to move the legs up, down, or side to side, puts unnecessary stress on the lower back. However, the same exercises may be done by positioning the body diagonally rather than straight back, slightly rounding the back and tightening the stomach muscles at the same time. Any leg movement downward will now be tolerable. The best way to exercise with lower back problems is in a vertical position moving the legs in front of the body. Again: stomach muscles should be tight.

Using the pull buoy on each foot for additional water resistance should only be considered:

- after being used to water exercises.

- after having strengthened the back and stomach.

- if there are no back problems.

- having no ankle or foot problems.

- if in doubt, having consulted a physician prior to class.

Legs, Buttocks, Hips, Stomach

The greatest part of exercising in chest-deep water or deeper, is the total body involvement from the hips down, compared to land exercising, in which you work only with your own body weight. In the water you are constantly forced to tackle water resistance in every direction the body moves. This action in turn causes a unique chain reaction of the muscles from the toes up. Almost effortlessly, the body gets a treatment in toning and firming plus a gentle massage to make it perfect.

Muscle aches are not necessary following a workout if the

exercises are monitored wisely. The overachiever, of course, will most always get a body reaction, and may do her or himself more harm than good. The best results in water exercising are achieved by doing it continuously once started, and on a regular basis. People in their late seventies and even eighties are frequently found in pools enjoying the weightless movements. Struggling limbs on land become wonderfully active and rehabilitated in water.

Legs and Kicks

In the water, any kind of kick is effective to help strengthen the legs, including:

1. flutter kicks
2. breast stroke kicks
3. dolphin (mermaid) kicks
4. scissor kicks
5. bicycle kicks
6. cross-over kicks
7. straddle-kick press kicks (legs separate and press together)
8. heel kicks (single heel kick up toward back)
9. stride step kicks (alternating far forward and back)
10. "ballerina toe" kicks (toes turned forward)
11. flexed footed kicks (toes turned up)
12. "pigeon toe" kicks (toes turned inward)
13. "Charley Chaplin" kicks (toes turned outward)
14. "sea horse" kicks (both heels kick up toward back)

The force and tempo used with each of these kicks make a difference. For instance, a person may be using the same slow speed of movement month after month, even after the muscles have been strengthened, or long after the legs are used to the exercise. Now she or he is not really getting enough out of it. The heart rate is not increasing during this exercise, and the leg muscles don't really show any sign of additional firming. As a result, the common complaint from the exerciser will probably be something like "This exercise doesn't do a thing for me." This person is correct. This way, the exercise will not do a thing for her or him. However, after starting with a slow pace over a period of perhaps one or two weeks, or until the legs are used to the movement, and then gradually increasing speed and force, the full benefit of water exercising will be possible.

➡ Straight leg kicks used in any direction or in any body position in the water will not only benefit the legs, but also the hips and hip joints, buttocks, and abdominals.

➡ Bent leg kicks will strengthen the knees, and the inner and outer thighs.

➡ Kicks with flippers on the feet will benefit the entire body below the hips due to the force necessary to move them in the water, but also have an added benefit by helping to strengthen the ankles and shins.

➡ A fast kick of any type will increase the heart rate and even more so if both arms are actively moving to the rhythm of the legs.

Note: People with hip, knee, or ankle problems should remember to exercise only the hip, knee, or ankle in alignment with the whole leg from the hip down. Joints that were stressed and aching prior to exercising need to be strengthened as a whole unit first. (Out-of-position joints need to be avoided at all costs.)

Arms and Shoulders

While exercising in water and holding onto the pool side, facing the wall creates the least stress to the shoulders. However, a lot of activity involves the arms by holding on and keeping the body in control while moving the legs down, toward the back, or side to side. The upper arms benefit greatly during these activities. As soon as the body is turned sideways and only one hand holds onto the side, only that side will benefit. Therefore, all exercises in this position have to be repeated on the other side, with the equal amount of movements as well. This should be done for all exercises in the vertical position, as well as in a sideways laying position. Arm, shoulder, and upper torso muscles will be moderately involved during these activities.

The strain on the shoulders increases as soon as the back is turned to the wall, which requires a reverse arm stretch or an above-the-head grip, depending on the height of the poolside. Arthritic or sensitive shoulders may react negatively to these kinds of movements, and precautions should be taken. Substitute exercises may have to be considered, or the duration of these exercises may be shortened. Once the shoulders are strong enough, or are used to the unusual extension, full participation may be resumed. Deep-water exercising involves and develops every muscle in the body.

Cramps

Cramping of muscles in the water is not only very painful, but can also be dangerous. Foot, calf, thigh, or abdominal cramps while swimming in deep water can be the cause of panic and even drowning.

There are many different reasons for sudden cramping or involuntary spasms of the muscles while swimming or exercising in water, including

• immersion in cold water.

• overstretching a muscle or tendon group.

• vigorous exercising.

• fatigue.

• poor circulation.

• a too-tight strap while using the pull buoy on the foot.

• a too-tense grip while using the pull buoy in the hand.

If swimming in a confined area or a swimming pool, and a muscle or tendon group gets tight and a cramp occurs, the best methods of relief are:

- relaxing and stretching the afflicted body part.

- mild rubbing of the muscle for circulation.

- tight grip over the muscle until the muscle begins to relax.

- pushing the foot against a solid object (floor, poolwall).

- removal from water, wrapping foot or leg in a towel for warmth.

The same methods can be applied while swimming in open water (lake, river, pond, ocean) with the addition of these most important rules:

Don't swim alone. Do not panic.

Most often a cramp will begin to relax if the swimmer limbers the afflicted leg or foot and uses arm movements only. An abdominal cramp can be relaxed by stretching the body, going into a back-floating position extending both arms over-head, and once floating in this position, relaxing completely. The swimmer should then slowly work his or her way to safety. Vigorous stroking and kicking will most likely result in recurrence of the cramp.

Exercising by the poolside is the safest place for the person who knows he or she has a tendency for foot or leg cramps. Simply hold onto the wall and relax the leg totally when the muscles begin to get tight. If the pull buoy is the cause for cramping, remove it at once. When the cramp is gone, mild exercising can be continued by not tightening this particular leg (foot). Most of the time the cramp is triggered by tense movements during exercising.

3

Pregnant and Senior Exercisers

Exercising during pregnancy should only be considered with the physician's approval. All exercises should be performed in chest- to shoulder-deep water. For full water support, a floating belt should be used in deep water. If an individual did not exercise prior to becoming pregnant, or if she has not exercised on a regular basis, all movements should be done cautiously, with a minimum of stress and extension to the joints. Hopping and bouncing in water can only be done moderately and with an extra support under the stomach with both hands. In the more advanced stages of pregnancy, hopping and bouncing should be eliminated completely.

Submerging, diving, or any other breath-holding exercises are not recommended during pregnancy. Most doctors recommend not exceeding the target heart rate over 120-130 beats per minute during pregnancy. (A personal consultation with a physician is very important). Vigorous exercising with peak heart rate (120-130 counts) should not be extended over more than five minutes followed by a stationary or slower moving routine. The maternal body temperature at this stage should not exceed 92° Fahrenheit.

As soon as any of the exercises become stressful during any stage of pregnancy, they should be discontinued and replaced by movements that feel comfortable. If cramping of the legs occurs more than once in a while, a physician should be consulted.

Warning Signs During Pregnancy

A physician should be contacted if any or a combination of

the following symptoms should occur: shortness of breath, dizziness, faintness, palpitations, pains in the abdomen, back, pubic area, or when walking: spotting or bleeding, excess fluid drainage, or contractions. All exercises should be stopped and a physician consulted.

Senior Waterobics and Exercises

To be considered a *senior* can be depressing for a lot of people fifty-four years old or older. Most of these people are in the midst of prime activities at home and at work, and are physically active. Just because they have turned fifty-four years old, ready or not, they are now labeled: *Senior*. In the past this meant he or she was now "finished" with an active lifestyle and was expected to retire in front of the television set or behind knitting needles leading a sedentary life.

That is no longer the case. In this country, we probably have more physically active seniors than people in their twenties. Many people in their twenties don't yet realize that it is vitally important to be physically active and to stay in good shape. People in their fifties *do* know, and many do something about it. Once they have started, they will learn that they have no choice but to stay physically fit for the rest of their lives.

Self-discipline in staying active and eating the right foods is now as important as life itself. This is exactly why they are pursuing a lifestyle very different from the one they led when they were in their twenties, thirties, or even forties.

Water exercises are the best and most-recommended exercises by physicians. A water program should be started with the intent to strengthen the body first if a physically inactive life was led prior to now. After a higher level of physical fitness has been achieved, waterobics for seniors might be the next option.

A regular fast-paced waterobics program is great if the physical condition tolerates it. One needs to know his or her own limits at all times at any age, and act accordingly. Many times the attending physician will make suggestions regarding the physical activities of the individual. A general suggestion is to consult your physician before participating in any type of physical fitness program.

Special exercises for senior citizens

Standing in chest deep water, facing the poolside, both hands holding onto the wall:

Description: **Position, body benefit:**

1. *Toe/Heel*

    Alternate, lift heels, roll to toes, push heels down again.

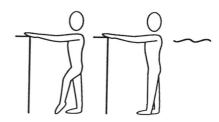

Calf, hamstring, shin

2. *Toes up*

    Alternate: on heels, toes up. Slightly bend, then straighten legs.

Calf, shin, thigh

3. *Roll heel to toes*

    Stand back from wall, with hands against wall. Simultaneously lean forward, keeping heels down, roll to toes. On the way up, return to heels.

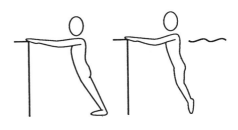

Calf, shin, thigh

4. *Hamstring*

Stand far back, but press heels down. Lean forward, in a push-up position (bend/straighten arms) without lifting heels. Back maintains straight, head up position.

Hamstrings

5. *Frog Squat*

Spread both legs, toes up, on heels only. Bend knees to maximum flexibility, straighten.

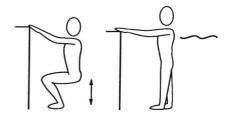

Shin, calf, inner thigh

6. *Pigeon toes*

Place both feet with toes in, spread feet slightly. Bend knees to touch, straighten legs.

Knee, thigh, calf

7. *Charleston*

Spread legs, on toes: lift heels, bend knees-simultaneously swing knees in/out.

Thigh, calf, shin

8. *Alice-flex*

Spread legs, turn feet out slightly. Bend knees, tuck in stomach, and tighten muscles. Lean back slightly, Move body up and down on toes, mildly bouncing.

Thigh, back, stomach

9. Alice-flex sway

Instead of straight up and down, shift weight left then right. Straighten out one leg, bend other.

Knee, thigh, back, stomach

4

Music and Exercise Tools

Music and Rhythm

The choice of music and rhythm to be used in water exercising has to be adapted to water movements and converted to allow participants to rhythmically follow along.

A normally slow musical rhythm will be too slow to use in water since all in-water movements are already slowed down. A normally fast musical rhythm will be too fast to be used in water for the same reason. Therefore, carefully chosen music with the correct tempo to accompany the water exercises is very important.

Examples of music that could be used:

Warm up: *Venus*
Hop/leap/jump: *Get out of my dreams*
Jogging: *King Creole*
Broomstick: *Let's Dance*
Pool side: *Bad Boys, La Bamba, Queen of the Hop, Rock n Roll Girl, La Isla Bonita*

Handweights: *Freeway of Love*
Kicking across the pool: *65 Love Affair*
Stomach/back exercises: *Conga*
Cooling down: *Girls just want to have fun*

Exercise Tools

The body is already working with a great exercise tool—water. Water provides resistance while the body moves back and forth, side to side, or up and down. The more speed that is applied, the more resistance results. With each and every move in the water, a combination of muscle groups and tendons is needed to make such a move possible.

In addition, water makes us feel light and weightless. In fact, the farther the body is submerged, the more buoyant the body becomes. Buoyancy means weightlessness. Buoyancy allows for low-impact movements in water. Buoyancy encourages arm and leg movements. Trying to get from point A to point B within a certain time span calls for even greater arm and leg activity. At this moment the body is the sole exercise tool.

To enhance exercising in water, an abundance of different, or *additional* tools can be used to encourage and increase muscle involvement. The most commonly used tools found around swimming pools might be:

1.   The kickboard to improve kicking
2.   The pull buoy to improve kicking or stroking
3.   Hand pads to improve stroking
4.   Ball (preferably volleyball size)

Hand pads and pull buoys increase muscle involvement

These are good tools to help strengthen arm, leg, back, and abdominal muscles, as well as help to improve endurance. In addition to these tools, the following equipment can be used to enhance kicking and/or torso flexibility:

- Small rustproof hand weights

- Wrist or ankle weights

- Weight belt

- Broomstick or dowel bar

- Rope/ribbon (different length)

- Flex band (soft elastic band of different length)

Any of the above-mentioned tools can be used for various exercises during any type of water fitness program in addition to the body (arm/leg) movements. The level of fitness plays a great part in choosing additional equipment to avoid overworking certain muscle groups.

Additional weight will increase the difficulty of kicking or arm movements. The addition of the pull buoy in the hands while submerged will strengthen arms, legs, back, and abdominals. The addition of the broomstick, flex band, or ribbon/rope enhances upper torso and shoulder flexibility,while improving arm extension. The addition of a rigid, standard size kickboard can be very effectual in stimulating the heart rate, inner thigh, and torso flexibility, as well as arm, leg, and torso muscles.

Broomsticks

Exercising with the broomstick helps increase shoulder and arm flexibility. With the aid of the broomstick, a maximum arm extension can be reached. This can be done easily in water as well as on land by extending both arms overhead, holding the stick on either end. The leg position has to be in a comfortable straddle position (feet apart) for balance. Elbows are locked in, arms are overhead and you are ready to bend the upper torso left to right or forward and back, or with the upper torso bend forward (flat back position) from side to side.

A half-body turn left to right is a great way to firm the inner thighs as well as raise the heart rate to a peak if performed in the water with a powerful upward hop with each body turn. You can get the full benefit of this exercise only in the water, since you're pushing your body off the ground with the power of your toes, turning your body in one move to the opposite direction while elevated, landing on your toes again with the front leg bent and the rear leg in an extended position. For maximum arm/shoulder flexibility, the broomstick should be held with the arms fully extended turned overhead toward the back.

Note: People with back problems should avoid any twisting or arching of the back.

Kickboards

A firmly textured kickboard is needed to help reach the desired effect while exercising in the water. For water exercises, the kickboard should be turned long-sided and held firmly on each edge. The board should be used by broad-siding it against the water pressure, and using powerful arm movements forward and back in a push and pull action, either:

1.   in front of the body,
2.   sideways to the body, or
3.   up and down in front of the body.

An effective water-resistance action will involve muscles in the upper arms, shoulders, chest, back, stomach, and upper thighs. During kickboard exercises, the legs are either together or in a straddled position (feet apart) to counterbalance the arm movements.

All kickboard action in front of the body requires a leg position with the feet close together and the knees flexible. All kickboard action to the side of the body requires a leg position with the feet apart and the body weight shifting from side to side.

The water depth for the exerciser should be waist deep to

facilitate bending or spreading the legs for the most effective results in both upper torso and thighs.

The Pull Buoy

The pull buoy set is made of two short foam cylinders connected by a nylon belt or rope and buckle for adjustments. The pull buoy with the nylon belt is the kind most suitable for water exercises, while the kind with the nylon rope is mostly preferred by swimmers.

The belted pull buoy is to be used in pairs, one for each hand, or one for each foot. The belt has to be adjusted in each case to fit the grip of the hand or the in-step of the foot.

For the hands

The cylinders have to be far enough apart to allow the hand to reach both belts(ropes). With the submerged pull buoy, the arm should always be slightly bent. The arm can then be pressed against the resistance of the water forward and back, by turning the wrist each time against the force of the water. Also any pressing action can be done from side to side or up and down, even circling around.

While using the pull buoy in the water, the exerciser can be:

The pull buoy in the hands is used for arm and chest strengthening

1.   Standing up in waist-, chest-, or shoulder-deep water. The legs should be together and bent, or apart with the body weight shifting from side to side as needed.
2.   The exerciser may also work in deep water in a vertical position with arm movements. The legs may be resting or actively moving with the arm rhythms.
3.   The exerciser may be laying on the stomach, pressing the arms downward below the chest.
4.   The exerciser may be laying on the back, pressing the arms backwards below the back.
5.   For kicking exercises laying on the stomach, back, or sideways, the arm with the pull buoy is extended forward, sideways, or near the body.

The pull buoy on the foot

The belt has to be adjusted so the foot can step in between the two foams held by the belt. One of the belts must be on top of the foot and the other belt must be on the bottom. The belt must be tight enough for the pull buoy to stay on the foot while submerged, but not so tight as to stop circulation and cause cramping of the foot.

Caution: The pull buoy's natural move will be up, since its consistency is lighter than water. The first-time user will have to hold onto the wall with both hands facing the wall.

Correct placement of the foot in the pull buoy

The body position has to be vertical until the exerciser is used to the pull buoy on the feet. Looking down, the exerciser should see his or her feet. If the feet move back, or to either side too far, the power of the pull buoy will make the body float up, and the exerciser will temporarily lose control. Simple steps and moves should be practiced first, until the legs are strong enough to control the pull buoy.

The exercises can be done:

- Vertically, holding onto the wall, or in the more advanced stages, free of the wall. The body should always be deep enough so that the feet cannot touch the bottom of the pool.

- Front floating position, holding onto the wall with both hands.

- Back turned to the wall, holding on backwards to the wall.

With the help of the pull buoy on the feet, a combination of muscles are strengthened at the same time: foot, calf, knee, inner and outer thigh, buttocks, hip, stomach, waist, upper torso, as well as arm and shoulder, from holding onto the wall.

Caution: people with back problems of any kind should not arch or twist the upper torso while exercising or using the pull buoy on the feet.

Hand weights in and out of the water

Hand weights must be easy to hold, and they need to be rustproof if they are to be used in water. They can be anything from commercial hand weights to plastic bottles, any size of canned goods up to 16 oz. (vegetables, fruit, etc.) after the labels have been removed. However, glass items or other breakable materials should never be used in the water, nor should pop or beer cans.

Hand weights should not exceed two pounds

The weight to be used depends entirely on the user's arm and shoulder condition. In general, 16 oz. or less is a pretty good size to start with. Gradually increase this weight as the muscles in the upper arms and shoulders get stronger.

A two lb. maximum weight in each hand for women is enough to work with over a long period of time, and still continue to improve the muscles in the wrists, arms, shoulders, back, and chest. Since all hand weight exercises are performed to a certain musical rhythm or tempo, it is unwise to exceed this weight. Shoulder, back, or elbow injuries may occur if hand weights are too heavy for the exerciser's physical condition.

The most effectual way to use hand weights during water exercises is by submerging the weights. By turning the palms against the water pressure with each move, the inner and outer arms are exposed to equal water resistance. The greater the pressure, the more muscle strength is required.

Hand weights out of the water (in the air) involve only the weight itself plus the weight of the arm. A lot of people prefer to use in- and out-of-the-water hand weight combination exercises. This creates a variety of moves and effects that cannot be matched in any other types of fitness programs. Hand weights can also be substituted with hand paddles or finned gloves, which are available in most indoor and outdoor pools. However, if one does not want to hold anything at all, a very good effect is achieved by simply opening the hands in the water with the fingers straight and together, while performing the suggested hand weight exercises.

The most effective use of hands weights is submerged

All of the mentioned methods are very effective in the water, and help diminish undesired dimples in upper arms. They help to firm and shape the arms in a similar way as by using exercise machines. However, there is one significant difference when exercising in the water: the entire body is working against water resistance, which automatically involves every muscle in the body.

Which exercises are to be used?

Nearly all warm-up exercises involving arm movements can be converted into hand weight exercises to be used for the arms both in and out of the water. To involve the stomach muscles at the same time, the stomach should be tucked in, and the legs should be flexible during the entire exercise period.

A good substitute hand weight

5

The Instructor

With each new waterobics class, the instructor has to show her or his sense of humor and even temperament. Getting involved yourself, and having fun doing the exercises with the class is very important. Personal problems must be set aside and not be shown during class. A boring instructor will have an unenthusiastic class. An instructor full of inspiring fire will have a willing and excited class.

By using a multitude of exercises, an enthusiastic instructor can make his or her students forget their daily problems and be totally committed to "their" class for the next forty-five or sixty minutes. And this is exactly what exercising is all about. May it be in a gym, on a dance floor, on the field, or in the water, exercising should be fun, it should help you let your hair down, and get you completely involved in what you are doing. When the class time is over, you should have the feeling that you have done something worthwhile, but the time went by too fast. Start out a new program with a set series of exercises, but as soon as the class has outgrown them, change within the same session to another variety of similar exercises. It will keep the students on their toes, and will make them want to come back to find out what you have planned for them today. It is easy to do and fun for the instructor, too.

If you have a very young group, you may want to use more of the faster-paced skills. If you have a senior or therapeutic group, there is an abundance of skills to choose from to accommodate their needs. If you have a mixed group of young to middle-aged people, heavy and slim, vigorous, and slow yet willing, by all means introduce anything from slow to faster skills and let them have fun at their own pace. It is very unprofessional to simply overlook the problems of slower students. Ask them to work at their own pace until they can cope with the rest of the class.

The ideal situation is to have divided levels including beginners, intermediates, and advanced. But this is not always possible. The only groups that can be separated from a regular waterobics class are the seniors. These students will need their own programs tuned to their needs and pace. Therefore it is important to adjust to the different capabilities and present your program as professionally as possible, with your expertise and knowledge guiding you through each class. It is important to be able to tackle any class situation at all times.

Class Structure

The fundamentals for a typical waterobics class should consist of four divisions:

1.   Warming up
2.   Upper torso flexibility and stretching
3.   The main section: working in deep water
4.   Tapering off and cooling down

Sections 1 and 2 should be done in hip- to chest-deep water.
Section 3 should always be done in deep water.
Section 4 may be done again in hip- to chest-deep water or by the wall.

With this basic formula, each instructor can create his or her own routines depending on the pool size, class advancement, and size of the class. In the beginning of each class, before starting any exercises, it is very important to check the heart rate. This may be taken at the wrist, or with minimum pressure, at the carotid pulse on one side of the Adam's apple (neck).

Once the starting heart rate has been established, the warming up exercises can be started. Due to different water temperatures in individual facilities, this part may be shortened or prolonged. In cold water, for instance, it is not a good idea to move slowly for a longer period of time. When the body is cold, the blood circulation is slowed down and the muscles stiffen. The result is a listless class, complaining of the water temperature. Increase the warming-up tempo as soon as possible. In warm water, the body movements should be slower when starting the class. Overexertion may occur quickly if the pace of the movements is too fast too soon.

The warming-up period should start out slowly, extending gradually into a faster-paced activity without interruption. After ten to fifteen minutes, the heart rate should be monitored immediately. At the end of the warm-up period, the heart rate should have reached the target count. (Each student should have been handed a sheet with written information about the target heart rate formula and should know his or her personal counts before starting a waterobics program). The second part of the class can start as soon as the body has been sufficiently warmed up.

Stretching and flexibility exercises should next be introduced to the class. Gradually the entire body will be included in the movements, starting with the arms, moving to the chest, waist, hips, thighs, and feet. No part should be left out. The time used for this section may be anywhere from ten to fifteen minutes long. For a forty-five minute class, part two may be ten minutes long.

The main part of the class will use the most amount of class time. All exercises should be introduced in deep water. Nonswimmers are urged to hold onto the poolside with both hands while exercising. For best results, the body has to be fully extended in a vertical position without touching the bottom of the pool. Floating belts are recommended for non- and weak swimmers.

The formula used for this part of the class is up to the individual instructor and the advancement of the participants. In general, a variety of basic exercises facing the wall can be used to start, and continued by turning the body in different positions toward the wall. In the advanced stages of exercising, additional water resistance equipment on the feet may be used to help strengthen the legs, stomach, back, and torso. However:

Caution is to be taken with flotation objects on the feet or ankles: it may be dangerous if an inexperienced student

uses this equipment without being able to control the body movements. Harmful twisting of the spine may occur.

A lap swimming period may be included into this section of the class structure to help increase stamina. The weak or nonswimmer should be allowed to follow the class pace with the support of a kickboard or a similar means of flotation. At the end of this period (which should not last longer than four minutes) a heart rate count is due.

Arm and upper torso strengthening exercises may follow the swimming part. Again, this can be done with very basic movements, and in the more advanced stages, kickboards and other hand tools may be added to further enhance the strengthening of the muscle structure. If time allows, an additional stomach muscle toning exercise should be included. This will conclude the main part of the waterobics class and the body will have to be allowed to slow down and cool off before the total time is finished.

To taper off, all students will meet once again in the shallow part of the pool, preferably in chest-deep water. All movements will have to be relaxing and slow-paced, and arms and legs should be limbered. Neck muscle stretches may be included in this section of the class. Before departing, a final heart rate count may be conducted to be sure that the heart rate has slowed down to the class beginning stage.

Suggested Class Outline

Exercise	Time
Warming up and stretching	4 to 5 minutes
Aerobic exercises	5 to 15 minutes

Now the body is warm enough to continue with:

Flexibility exercises	3 to 5 minutes

Endurance exercising, including swimming, jogging, hops, skips, and leaps forward, back or sideways	5 to 8 minutes
Facial and neck exercises	3 to 5 minutes
Group exercises (circle)	3 to 5 minutes
Cooling down	4 to 5 minutes

The suggested time is optional for the individual exercises. Some sections may require more and some less time, depending on the overall class fitness status.

6

Water Exercises With and Without Hand Tools

Warming Up and Cooling Down

These exercises are suitable for all progressions of physical fitness programs in the water. Some of the movements can be done holding hand weights or paddles or using finned gloves.

All students should be in hip- or chest-deep water when performing any of the warm-up or cool-down exercises suggested below. Students with any kind of shoulder problems will move to deeper water to be able to keep the shoulders submerged. Out-of-water exercises should then be substituted for in-water movements.

Mild on-the-spot jogging is recommended when the students have performed another kind of warming-up activity prior to this or if the water or air temperature is less than 80° Fahrenheit and more body movement is necessary to prevent chilling.

Options: Stand comfortably,
Do on-the-spot jogging, or
Increase tempo for cardiovascular benefits

Arms:

10. *Alternate shoulder lift*

    Both arms down to each side, lift one shoulder toward ear, drop other shoulder down, alternate.

11. *Double shoulder lift*

    Simultaneously lift both shoulders toward ears, drop down.

12. *Alternate arm stretch up*

    Fully extend one arm overhead, other arm bends, elbow touches hip.

13. *Double arm stretch*

    Simultaneously bend/extend up.

14. *Alternate shoulder touch*

    Arms shoulder high: one arm fully extends to side (palm up) other arm bends: fingertips touch shoulder.

15. *Double shoulder touch*

Simultaneously bend, extend up.

16. *Alternate chest touch*

Arms shoulder high, one arm fully extended to side (palm down), other arm bends, fingertips touch chest.

17. *Double chest touch*

Simultaneously bend, extend to side.

18. *Alternate elbow lift*

Both arms down to each side, lift one elbow shoulder high while other arm stays straight, alternate.

19. *Double elbow lift*

Simultaneously bend, extend down.

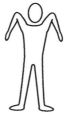

20. *Cross over*

   Cross both arms in front of
   body, separate arms to far
   side.

21. *Half arm swing*

   Extend both arms to far left,
   swing both arms across (in
   front) to far right, legs flexible.

22. *Alternate forward punch*

   Fists punch (fully extend)
   one arm forward, other
   arm bends, elbow draws
   back, alternate.

23. *Alternate forward press*

   Open hands (palms for-
   ward), one arm fully extended forward, other arm
   bends, elbow draws back,
   alternate.

24. *Open/close hand (high)*

   Both arms extended high,
   close one hand, open other,
   alternate.

25. *Open/close hand (side)*

Both arms shoulder high to each side: close one hand, open other, alternate.

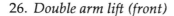

26. *Double arm lift (front)*

Both arms simultaneously swing (lift) forward and back, one foot steps forward, other foot back, legs flexible.

27. *Clap overhead*

Reach over the head and clap hands to rhythm of music.

28. *Reach behind head alternate*

Both arms fully extended overhead, bend one arm, reach behind head, keep other arm straight overhead, alternate.

29. *Arm swing (forward, back)*

One leg forward, other back, swing one arm far forward, other far back, alternate.

30. *Tuck, press arms*

Feet together, bend knees, tuck stomach. Press both arms forward (palms forward) then press both arms back to hips (palms back) knees flexible.

31. *Arch, press arms*

Feet separated, bend knees, arch back, head up. Both arms press back, (palms back) turn palms, press forward to hips.

32. *Elephant trunk*

Separate feet, bend knees, tuck stomach. Both hands clasp fingers, and arms swing to far left (head turns to same direction) Both arms swing to far right (head turns to same direction), legs flexible.

33. *Rainbow (overhead)*

Both arms fully extended overhead, cross arms overhead, lower toward shoulders (rainbow), legs flexible.

34. *Limber and shake*

Both arms are in the water, limber and shake hands.

35. *Shake, rattle and roll*

Lift feet off floor, limber kicks. Arms, limber, shake. Head moves in a comfortable rolling motion.

Facials and Neck:

36. *Tilt Head*

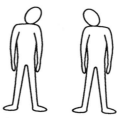

Head to left shoulder (ear first) tilt head to right shoulder (ear first).

37. *Pucker and tuck*

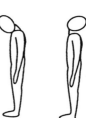

Stand comfortably, arms down, tuck chin to chest, lift chin and pucker up.

38. *Funny face*

Stand comfortably, arms down, form mouth as to say "oooo", then form mouth as to say "eeee" as far as you can.

39. *Jaws*

Stand comfortably, arms
down, move lower jaw to-
ward left, then move lower
jaw to right. Turn head to
each side.

40. *Neck stretch*

Stand comfortably, arms
down, drop head forward,
look down, turn head
slowly left and right.

Circles:

41. *Double circle (high)*

Both arms are up, clasp
fingers, draw big in air
overhead (change direc-
tion). Upper torso is in-
volved, legs separated,
shift weight.

42. *Single circle (high)*

One arm is up, other arm
is down, legs are separated,
flexible. Draw big circle in
air overhead (change di-
rection), upper torso in-
volved.

43. *Double circle (front)*

Separate legs, hands to-
gether, clasp fingers, draw
circle in front of body,
(tuck) shift weight.

44. *Single circle (front)*

Separate legs (squat position), one arm draws big
circle in front of body,
(change direction), other
arm down, alternate arms.

45. *Wrist circle (high)*

Both arms are overhead,
hands in fists, simulta-
neous wrist circles (change
direction.)

46. *Wrist circle (side)*

Both arms are fully ex-
tended to each side
(shoulder high). Hands in
fists, simultaneous wrist
circles (change direction).

Knees:

47. *Double knee twist*

Feet are together, bend
knees. Knees together, lift
up onto toes, twist knees
toward left, right, use arms
for balance.

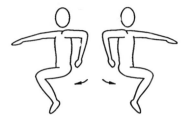

48. *Knees (bend/extend)*

Separate feet far apart, lift
up onto toes: bend knees,
knees touch, straighten
legs.

49. *Knee flops*

Separate feet far apart, lift
up onto toes, bend knees
apart, together.

50. *Deep knee bends*

Feet together, bend knees,
straighten. Lift onto toes,
both arms in front, (as in
standard knee bends).

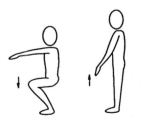

51. *Hee haw hop*

Separate feet, hop up at same time. Lift both knees up, out, and reach with both hands down toward inside of feet using the momentum of elevation, as feet come down, arms lift up (elbows high) shoulders back.

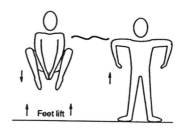

52. *Elbow/knee*

One foot down, opposite knee up. Elbow touches knee, alternate, rhythmical movements.

53. *Alternate knee lift*

(Slow or fast). Alternating knee lifts.

54. *Knee up, kick back*

(Slow or fast). Lift one knee up, extend leg toward back, alternate.

55. *Fire hydrant*

(Hold onto wall or stand free). Bend one knee, lift up sideways (hip high) foot points back, press knee down to touch other leg, alternate.

Legs:

56. *Kick forward*

(Slow or fast). One leg kicks far forward, alternate.

57. *Kick forward, reach*

(Slow or fast). One leg kicks far foward and high enough for the opposite hand to touch toes, alternate.

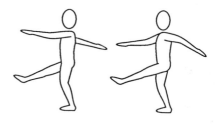

58. *Side kick*

(Slow or fast). One leg kicks out to one side, alternate.

59. *Cross over kick*

One leg crosses in front of the other and kicks (arms swing opposite to kick) alternate.

60. *Launch forward*

Both arms are up, one foot in front (bend knee). One foot far back (straight leg), arch back, alternate. Use rhythms of two or four before changing leg position.

61. *Launch sideways*

Squat down, extend one leg straight sideways, alternating leg shifts (arms stay shoulder high for balance). Use rhythms of one, two or four before changing leg position.

62. *Walk on heels*

Legs are flexible, lift toes as far as possible, walk forward on heels only.

63. *Walk on toes*

Lift up onto toes (both arms up), walk forward on toes only.

64. *Single leg bicycle*

(Hold onto wall or stand free) Stand on one leg, other leg bends, and foot draws bicycle motions forward or reverse, alternate.

65. *Rotate foot*

(Hold onto wall or stand free) Stand on one leg, other leg extends forward or to side and rotates foot at the ankle (change direction, alternate.

66. *Single leg lift*

(Hold onto wall or stand free) Stand on one leg, lift other leg up sideways (toes pointed or flexed), press straight down, alternate.

Torso bends:

67. *Torso bends*

    Spread legs, hands to waist, bend upper torso, left, right.

68. *Back bends*

    Legs are separated, hand to waist, arch back, bend knees, head back.

69. *Torso bends, arms up*

    Spread legs, both arms are overhead, clasp fingers, bend upper torso and arms left, right (weight shift on legs is optional).

70. *Hoola hoop*

    Feet are together, rotate hips in circular motion (change direction) arms out for balance.

71. *Torso twist*

Spread legs. One elbow is chest high in front, other arm reaches behind body (back). Shift weight from one leg to other as arms change position from front to back and upper torso twists. Rhythms of one, two or more can be used before arms change position.

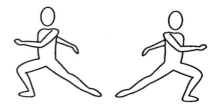

72. *One arm torso bend*

Spread legs. One arm is up reaching over top of head, other arm is bent in front of chest. Bend torso to side, extending front arm opposite the torso. Bend, alternate.

73. *Upper torso rotation*

Spread legs. Arms are up, clasp fingers. Rotate arms and upper torso at same time, shifting weight on legs, change direction.

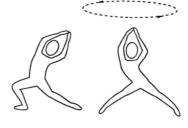

74. *Tuck forward*

Feet together, tuck, arms overhead, fingers down, limber forward, straighten up, hands to back.

75. *"Alice" tuck*

Spread legs and feet with knees turned out. Bend knees, tilt hips forward, lift up onto toes and use bouncing motions on the spot, forward or sideways. Abdominals and upper thighs very tight.

76. *Quick step*

(Slow or fast). Alternating forward and back steps (short or long steps). Arms overhead performing alternating forward and back movements opposite leg movements. (Options: arms bend, alternate presses forward, back, open hands or fists).

Note: All exercises requesting holding onto the wall can also be done in deep water (in the vertical position) with or without the pull buoy on each foot.

Poolside Exercises With and Without the Pull Buoy on Each Foot (All poolside exercises should be done in deep water so feet don't touch bottom. Body should be weightless.)

Description: ### Position, body benefit:

77. *Straddle press*

    Legs are straight, spread
    legs, press together, toes
    forward.

Inner thighs

78. *Charley Chaplin*

    See #77, feet are turned out,
    heels touch.

Buttocks, upper thighs

79. *Cross over*

    Cross legs left and right, as
    far as possible.

Waist, hips, thighs

80. *Stride step*

    Alternate forward and
    back, long steps.

Legs, thighs, stomach

81. *Quick step*

Alternate forward, back, short, fast step.

Thighs, stomach, back

82. *Leg circles*

Circle each leg in and out, small and big circles.

Legs, stomach, back

83. *Marching*

Alternate as in marching, legs move up and down.

Upper thighs, stomach

84. *Stomping*

Pull up both knees, push down both feet simultaneously.

Stomach, thighs

85. *Heel kicks*

   Legs are together, kick both
   heels up and down.

Stomach, thighs

86. *Pendulum*

   Legs are together, swing
   from waist down, left and
   right.

Stomach, back, waist

87. *Pendulum circles*

   See #86, circle legs left,
   right.

Stomach, back

88. *Kick out*

   Knees are up in front, lean
   left, right, kick both legs
   far out.

Waist, hips

89. *Knee twist*

Knees are up in front, lean left, then right, tilt both knees to left and right.

Waist

90. *Knee flop*

Knees are up in front, feet together, press knees out, in (open/close).

Stomach, thighs

91. *Mountain climber*

One foot is against wall, far up, other foot is against wall extended far down. Alternate step up, down.

Hamstring, stomach, back

92. *Calorie shaker*

Both feet are far up against wall, kick legs back together, fully extend body, pull feet back to wall.

Hamstring, stomach, back

93. *Calorie shaker, straddle back*

See #92, Pull both legs back straddled (far apart), unite back at wall.

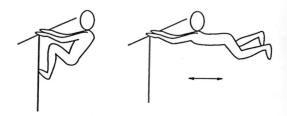

Inner thighs, back, stomach

94. *Calorie shakers, turn*

See #92, turn body sideways, kick legs left, pull up, turn body sideways, kick legs right, pull up.

Waist, thighs, back, stomach

95. *Bicycle*

Alternate bicycle step forward, back.

Inner, outer thighs

Facing the Wall

Description: **Position, body benefit:**

96. *Step down*

    Legs together, alternate step far down, left, right leg.

Stomach, back

97. *Straddle presses*

    Legs are together, spread apart. Press together, with long, slow presses and short, fast presses.

Inner thighs, back

98. *Criss-cross*

    Legs are slightly bent, cross left and right, long and slow. Legs cross left/right, short/fast.

Waist, stomach, back

99. *Butterfly or Mermaid kick*

    Legs are together, point toes, bend knees slightly, kick feet (rolling leg motion).

Legs, back

100. *Frog kick*

Feet curl up and touch, legs
circle out, then feet curl up
and touch.

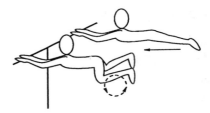

Thighs

101. *Kick heels*

Legs are together, bent.
Alternate, kicking heels up,
down.

Thighs

102. *Flutter kicks*

Legs are together, straight.
Alternate kicking legs up
and down.

Legs, cardiorespiratory

103. *Lift up*

Legs are together, straight.
Alternate, lifting out of
water, left and right.

Back, stomach

104. *Knee tucks*

Legs are together, straight. Tuck knee, alternate, left and right.

Back, stomach

105. *Double press*

Legs are together, straight. Press both legs down, then up.

Stomach, back

Laying Sideways

107. *Stride step*

Alternate legs forward and back, long steps.

Upper thighs, stomach

108. *Clap-clap*

Legs are together, straight, straddle and press together.

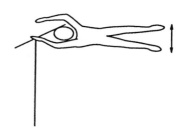

Upper thighs, stomach

109.   *Lift out*

Legs are together and straight. Upper leg lifts out of water and down.

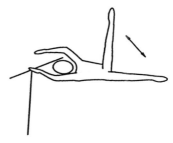

Upper thighs

110. *Fire hydrant*

Knees are together, bend legs. Upper knee, foot lifts out of water and down.

Inner thighs

111. *Double side press*

Legs are together and straight. Press both legs down at same time, (only as far as hip moves).

Back

112. *Side flutters*

Legs are together and straight. Alternate flutter kicks.

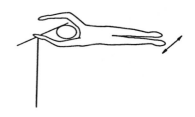

Thighs, buttocks

113. *Side butterfly (mermaid)*

Legs are together, moderately bent, double leg kick, bend.

Thighs

114. *Double heel kick*

Legs are together, bend knees, double kick toward back. Straighten both legs.

Thighs

115. *Side heel kick*

Legs are together, alternate kick toward back.

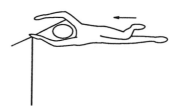

Thighs

116. *Side knee lift*

Legs are together, alternate knee lift, extend.

Thighs

Back to the Wall

Hold on backwards to wall, deep enough so feet don't touch
bottom of pool, both hands holding on backwards to the wall.
Lean forward until the chin touches the water and the arms are
straight, buttocks are close to wall. Legs are far down or moving
up, side in front of the body. Do with or without pull buoy on
each foot. Point or flex toes during exercises.

Description: **Position, body benefit:**

117. *Knee lift*

     Alternate up and down
     knee lifts, press straight
     down.

Stomach

118. *Double knee lift*

     Both knees lift up, press
     straight down.

Stomach

119. *Straight lift*

     Alternate straight legs,
     forward, up and down.

Stomach, upper thighs

120. *Straddle press*

Legs are straight down, straddle apart, press together. Option: short step or long step.

Stomach, thighs

121. *Criss cross*

Legs are straight down, straddle apart, cross over. Option: short step or long step.

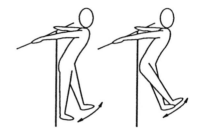

Stomach, thighs

122. *Leg circle*

Legs are straight down, legs circle simultaneously. Option: circle in or out.

Stomach, thighs

123. *Sitting circle*

Legs are straight forward, making simultaneous circles. Option: out/down/up, or circle in/down/up.

Stomach, thighs

124. *Sitting straddle*

Legs are straight forward. Straddle apart, press together, far up.

Stomach, thighs

125. *Sitting Press*

Legs are straight forward, both legs press down, lift up.

Stomach, back

126. *Charley Chaplin*

Legs are straight down, toes turned out. Option: Alternate forward, back steps or straddle,press. Heels touch, short steps.

Stomach, thighs

Bicycle kicks or treading water with or without pull buoys on feet

Beginner students need to hold onto the wall (deep water). Advanced students do the free style across the pool in deep water. Option: students may hold pull buoys in each hand or hold onto a kickboard for additional support.

Description: **Position, body benefit:**

127. *Bicycle kick forward*

Body in vertical position. Alternate legs, feet bicycle, forward, and down. Option: follow the wall and hold on, or free style.

Stamina, legs

128. Bicycle kick reverse

See #127. Reverse, alternate bicycle kicks.

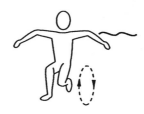

Stamina, thighs

129. Treading water

Body in vertical position, forward/back, or side to side. Slightly circular kicks (with pull buoys on feet side to side kick is not circular) Option: adding additional weight with arms out of the water.

Stamina, legs

Pull buoys in hands

Body in a vertical position (deep water), stationary movements. A set of pull buoys always means two cylinders connected by rope or nylon belt. See photographs.

130. *The hop*

Arms are extended to each side. Option: arms submerged. Hop forward and back, over imaginary hurdle. Feet stay together, arms move opposite legs.

Stomach, legs

131. *Side kick*

Arms are extended to each side. Pull both knees up before both legs kick far up to each hand, body tilts left, then right, cheek touches the water.

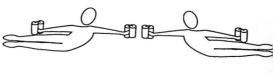

Stomach, waist

132. *Criss-cross*

See #121. Arms extended to each side.

Stomach, waist, legs

133. *Run-run*

Arms are extended to each side. Option: arms submerged. Legs perform alternated simulated running action.

Stamina, legs

134. *Swinger*

Arms are extended to each side. Option: arms submerged.
1. Pull up both knees, kick foward, tilt body back.
2. Pull up both knees, kick back, tilt body forward.

Stomach, back

135. *Rock the cradle*

Arms are extended to each side. Option: arms submerged. In sitting position, legs are straight, together, hold. Swing hips far back, far forward, legs stay in front at all times.

Stomach

136. *Double circle*

Arms are extended to each side, legs are straight, together. Circle both, left and right.

Stomach, waist

Pull Buoys in Hands: Laying Front, Side, Back

Description: **Position, body benefit:**

137. *Flutter kick*

Arms are together, forward in a prone body position, fast flutter kicking.

Stamina, legs

138. *Side flutters*

Laying on one side, upper arm   is extended down, lower arm is extended forward. Cheek in water. Fast flutter   kicking sideways, change sides.

Stomach, waist, legs

139. *Back flutters*

Lay on the back, both arms extended straight overhead, fast flutter kicking.

Stomach, legs

140. *Butterfly (Mermaid)*

Lay on stomach, both arms extended straight forward. Legs together, bend, kick, slightly submerged.

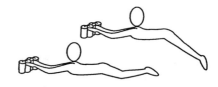

Stomach, back, legs

141. *Butterfly kick backwards*

Laying on the back, arms on each side of body, head up. Legs together, bend, kick, slightly submerged.

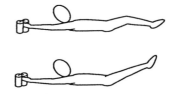

Stomach, neck, legs

142. Breast stroke kick

Laying on stomach, both arms extended forward. Feet, knees together, bend knees, circle feet out together. (Knees will separate when feet circle out). Option: can be performed laying on the back, both arms extended overhead.

Caution: May be harmful to sensitive knees.

Legs

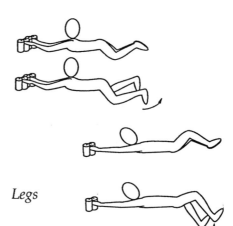

Group Fun Exercises

Group fun exercises in deep water (for swimmers only). Non-swimmers need to hold onto flotation device. Students form a circle by holding onto each others' hands. Depending on the number of students several circles may have to be formed (ten to fifteen people per circle).

Description: **Position, body benefit:**

143. *The Star*

One set of pull buoys is in right hand, close circle. Keep arms straight to sides, lay on back. Spread legs, touch neighbors' feet inside the circle.

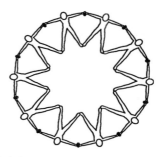

Spirit

144. *Motorboat*

One set of pull buoys is in right hand, close circle. Keep arms straight to sides, lay on stomach, legs back, kick. Blow bubbles (optional).

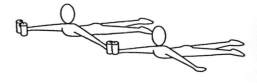

Spirit, legs

145. *Merry-go-round*

One set of pull buoys is in right hand. Close circle, keep arms straight. Lay on right side, side flutters, change sides.

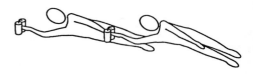

Spirit, legs, waist

146. *Fountain*

One set of pull buoys is in right hand, close circle. Lay on back, legs inside circle, vigorous kicks, splashes.

Caution: if less than ten people to a circle, kicking is dangerous.

Stamina, legs

147. *"Ring around" in deep water*

One set of pull buoys is in right hand, close circle. Vertical body position, "run-run" toward right side, change toward left side.

Stamina, legs

148. *Pointer*

One set of pull buoys is in right hand, close circle. Lay on back, legs inside circle. Lift up right leg, hold, lift up left leg, hold.

Upper thighs

149. *Can-can*

One set of pull buoys is in right hand, close circle. Lay on back, legs inside circle. Lift up right leg, kick up, down. Lift up left leg, kick up, down.

Upper thighs

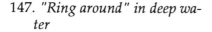

Group Circle Exercises

Group exercises are performed in a circle in hip or chest deep water. They can be performed forward, backward, or side to side. Depending on the number of students, several circles may have to be formed (ten to fifteen people per circle). Direction of movement changes frequently.

Description: **Position, body benefit:**

150. *"Ring-around" in shallow water*

Hold onto neighbors' hands, close circle.

1. jog left, right
2. skip left, right
3. hop left, right
4. leap sideways left, right

Change direction frequently.

Cardiovascular

Kickboard Exercises

Standing in hip or chest deep water, hold the kickboard broadside with one hand on each side. Accommodate each arm movement with body flexibility, tighten leg and stomach muscles. When the exercise calls for a straddle position, squat as far down as possible with each arm movement for the most possible inner thigh effect.

Description:	Position, body benefit:

151. *Waves*

Feet are together, bend knees, board should be broadside, half submerged. Move forward, then back in front of body (push/pull).

Stomach, back, arms

152. *Under current*

One foot steps back, hold board broadside, submerge. Move forward, then back, in front of body (push/pull).

Stomach, back, arms

153. *Push/pull sideways*

Spread legs, shift weight. Board should be broadside, half submerged. Turn body right, push/pull. Board toward the right, turn body left, push/pull board to left.

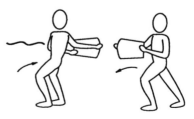

Stomach, legs, arms

154. *Washboard*

Feet are together, bent.
Board should be flat, hold
onto each side, press down,
lift out high. Tilt board to
let water run away from
you.

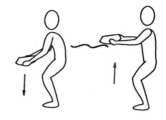

Stomach, back, arms

155. *Big Dipper*

Spread legs, shift weight.
Hold board longside, dip
in (left hand first) on far
right side, guide under-
water to far left side. Repeat in other direction.

Stomach, inner thighs

156. *The big splash or water fight*

Spread legs, shift weight.
Hold board broadside,
lower edge submerged.
Press board powerfully
from far right across water
to far left. Without releas-
ing board, turn to power-
ful press in other direction,
causing a fountain of wa-
ter to spray the nearest
neighbor each time you
press.

*Cardiovascular, arms, legs,
stomach*

Cardiovascular Exercises Across the Pool

These exercises should be done in hip- or chest-deep water, moving across the pool as fast as possible. Move arms forward and back in (or upward out of) the water.

Description:	**Position, body benefit:**

157. *Jogging across forward*

Jog forward across the pool, at a fast pace, arms move rhythmically.

Cardiovascular, legs

158. *Running across backward*

Run backwards across pool at a fast pace. Arms press forward alternately (monitor your direction).

Legs

159. *Leap forward*

Leap forward, left leg and right, legs, arms reach far up with each leap.

Cardiovascular

160. *Bunny hop*

Feet are together, hop forward, arms submerged. Press arms back with each hop.

Cardiovascular, legs

161. *Butterfly*

Feet are together, hop forward. Arms perform the butterfly stroke with each hop.

Cardiovascular, legs

162. *Side leap*

Long leap sideways, arms are shoulder high, spread out. Bend in rhythm with each leap (fingers touch).

Cardiovascular, legs

163. *Hop scotch*

Feet are together, hop sideways. Arms press in and out in rhythm with each hop.

Cardiovascular, legs

164. *Leap scotch combining side leap, hop scotch*

Alternate side leap, hop scotch using proper arm movements.

Cardiovascular, legs

165. *Cross country*

As in cross country skiing: alternate locked in leg movements, forward and back with a hop. Alternate opposite arm presses under water or overhead.

Cardiovascular, legs

166. *Watusi*

Feet are together, bent (shoulders submerge). Hop far up and forward, arms move far up with each hop.

Cardiovascular, legs

Broomstick (rope) exercises

Standing in hip- or chest-deep water, hold the broomstick with arms fully extended as close to each end of the stick as possible. Hold the rope fully extended on each end. The legs are spread and depending on which direction the arms move, one leg will always be straight and the other bent. For the hop and turning movements, the toes will be used to help elevate the body, and the stick (rope) will be used as the momentum to turn the body in the opposite direction. Physical ability and strength of the individual is a prime factor for reaching higher or greater speed in turning, none of which should be overdone and should be executed only within the limits of the instructor's suggested tempo and rhythm. For any of the body turns, the body should never be twisted from the waist up, the body should turn *as a whole unit, with a shift of weight on the legs.*

Description:

Position, body benefit:

167. *Torso bend*

Legs are straddled, both arms straight overhead. Bend torso once or twice to each side.

Torso, arms, flexibility

168. *Torso circle*

Legs are straddled, both arms straight overhead. With stick (rope) and arms in same position, draw circle in the air. Upper torso rotates, weight shift on legs.

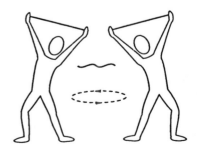

Abdominals, back, flexibility

169. *Body turns*

Legs are straddled, both arms straight overhead. With stick (rope) and arms in same position, half turn toward each side, feet stay in same position, weight shift on legs.

Torso, back, flexibility

170. *Front, back flex*

Legs are straddled, arms extended overhead. Lower both arms hip high toward front. Raise both arms overhead, toward back, shoulder high. Feet stay in same position. On the spot jogging possible.

Arm, shoulder flexibility

171. *Hop, turns up*

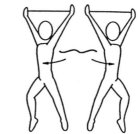

Before each turn, use toes to push body up for the hop. Weight shift on legs.

Cardiovascular, feet, legs, torso

172. *Hop, turns front*

Arms are extended forward, head turns opposite the arm movement. Weight shift on legs.

Cardiovascular, feet, legs, torso

173. *Hop, turns back*

See #170 for movement. Arms are extended backwards. Arms move in back, right to left, and left to right.

Cardiovascular, feet, legs, arms

174. *Side launch*

Legs are straddled far, arms extended overhead. Torso, arms, stick (rope) stay in same position, while weight shifts left to right (right to left) on legs.

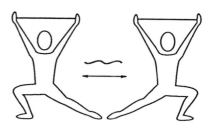

Inner thighs, torso flex

175. *Launch up*

One leg is straight far back, other leg bends forward. Arms extended overhead, pressing back. Arch back, switch leg position, one or two arm presses on each side.

Inner thighs

175 a. *Launch/tuck*

See leg position, #175. Arms extended far forward. Head between arms, deep launch. One or two repetitions on each side.

Inner thighs, back flex

175 and 175a can be combined for forward and upward movements.

176. *Limbo hop*

Legs are straddled, knees bent, body leans back, arms extended forward (chest high). With head up or back, toes push body upward into hopping movements forward and backward, only the feet move.

Upper thighs, abdominals, neck

Broomstick exercises in waist to chest deep water allow for upper torso flexibility

7

Submerging Exercises

A combined exercise above and under water is another form of stimulating the cardiorespiratory system. By deeply inhaling above water and exhaling just before or while surfacing, oxygen is pumped into the lungs in faster intervals if the exercise is repeated several times in a row. Leg and arm action will enhance the exercise. Again, we are dealing with a multiple body strengthening exercise. If upon the inhale, a deep squatting movement follows, combined with leg and arm pressing in order to surface, the arm action may be started above the head followed by a simultaneous arm press down toward the hips. The arm action may also be started shoulder high or lower, followed by a simultaneous arm press toward the hips or continuing toward the front (back) of the body.

The leg action will take place in an alternating or simultaneous move with either the feet together, one leg in front (bent) the other leg back (straight) as in the "mountain climber" exercise (see: facing the pool-side exercises), side to side, or single leg activity.

A.   Stationary shallow water submerging exercises may be performed in a depth of three to five feet.
B.   Moving forward submerging exercises in shallow water may be performed in a depth of three to five feet.
C.   Deep water submerging exercises may be performed in a depth six feet or deeper depending on the person's height.

All underwater exercises should always be done in clear water with every participant moving in the same direction at the same time. Submerging exercises should only be repeated up to five times in a row for beginners, up to 10 times for intermediate students, and no more than 15 times for advanced students. If dizziness or lightheadedness occurs, all exercising must be stopped and a relaxing period should follow, combined with periodic heart rate monitoring.

Women in any stage of pregnancy should only perform submerging exercises with a doctor's approval. Those with heart conditions, respiratory conditions, inner ear conditions or taking medication that causes drowsiness should only submerge if they have a doctor's approval. *If in doubt: do not submerge.*

Description: ## Position, body benefit:

177. *Beginner squat*

   Face the wall, hold on with both hands. Feet down, inhale, submerge, 3-5 repetitions.

Cardiorespiratory

178. *Deep squat*

   Inhale, submerge to a deep squat. Feet are together or apart. Arms shoulder high in front, press down during surfacing, 3 to 10 repetitions.

Legs, cardiorespiratory

179. *Cossack squat*

   Inhale, submerge, with feet apart. Kick with heel down to right. Surface, inhale, submerge. With feet apart, kick heel down left. Surface, arms shoulder high to each side, press down, 3 to 10 repetitions.

Inner thighs, cardiorespiratory

180. *Squat step*

Inhale, submerge. With feet together, extend right leg forward, surface.

Hamstring, cardiorespiratory

181. *Flip side*

Inhale, lay on right side. Kick both legs out, pull knees up. Inhale, flip to left side, kick both legs out (fully extended). Both arms in front, chest high. Shift with each flip, 5-15 repetitions.

Waist, cardiorespiratory

Submerging forward and up movements in shallow water (depth of 3-5 feet).

Leg position:

1. together, squat, press forward and up.
2. "mountain climber" position, press forward, up, alternate leg position.
3. Stride leg position (forward, back), alternate leg position.

Description: **Position, body benefit:**

182. *Mountain climber*

Inhale, submerge. One leg
is in front (bent), one leg is
straight back. Powerful leg
press forward and up.
Surface, repeat with alternate leg position. Arms
forward, shoulders high,
press down, back. Five to
10 repetitions.

Legs, cardiorespiratory

183. *Mountain climber*

See # 182. Arms are over-
head, press down to each
side. Five to 10 repetitions.

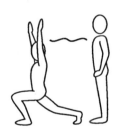

Legs, cardiorespiratory

184. *The hop- A*

Legs are together, inhale,
submerge. Powerful hop
forward, up. A- arms for-
ward, shoulder high.

Legs, cardiorespiratory

185. *The hop-B*

B- Arms down to each side.

Legs, cardiorespiratory

186. *The hop-C*

C- Arms in back.

Legs, cardiorespiratory

187. *The hop - D*

D- Arms overhead.

Legs, cardiorespiratory

188. *The hop - E*

E- Butterfly arms stroke.

Legs, cardiorespiratory

189. *Split-pop*

Inhale, submerge. Extend one leg as far forward as possible, one leg as far back as possible, press together. Surface, alternate leg position, arms press from side down. Five to 10 repetitions.

Inner thighs, cardiorespiratory

Submerging in deep water

In water 6-10 feet deep, use the following body position:

1. vertical
2. arms, head first (surface dive)

Upon the inhale both arms lift out of the water overhead while the body submerges to desired depth or until both feet touch the bottom. If feet don't touch the bottom, a simultaneous arm/leg pressing-kicking action is needed to surface. If feet touch the bottom, both legs bend and with a powerful leg/arm pressing action, the body will be elevated to the surface. Both arms overhead pressing down will increase the surfacing speed.

When performing a surface dive and continuing to swim forward underwater, it is up to the individual's underwater tolerance as to how deep he or she wants to swim and how many arm strokes can be performed according to breath-holding capacity. Personal safety and well being should be the first priority.

Description: **Position, body benefit:**

190. *Deep water bobbing, touch down*

Inhale, both arms over-head, submerge. Touch bottom, surface with powerful arm/leg press. Five to 10 repetitions.

Cardiorespiratory

191. *Deep water bobbing, stride kick*

See #190. As arms press down, legs separate for-ward, and back. Powerful leg press together. Option: flutter kicking. Five to 10 repetitions.

Cardiorespiratory

192. *Surface dive*

Inhale, submerge with arms overhead, head first (reverse body position) to desired depth. Level body, continue to swim under-water, forward and up to surface. Five to 10 repeti-tions.

Cardiorespiratory

8

Exercising in Shallow Water

The most ideal pools for swimming lessons, water exercises, and also waterobics are pools with a beach-type water entrance starting from zero, gradually sloping into deeper levels and ending with a water level of perhaps 10 feet. This situation is usually found in wave pools across the United States and in European countries. Indoor wave pools are the perfect places for physical water fitness activities.

Most sitting, laying, squatting, or kneeling land exercises can be performed in these body positions as long as the water reaches the shoulders. This will give the body enough buoyancy to make it possible to float while the finger tips are still touching the bottom of the pool. Even if you could never do a push-up on land it is now possible to do ten, twenty, or more in a row without any problems. While doing any kind of kneeling exercises, it is best to keep a towel under the knees to prevent any scraping or bruising of the knees.

Caution: elderly and very heavy exercisers might have difficulty maintaining a good balance while sitting or laying in shallow water.

Sitting in Shallow Water

While sitting in shallow water and exercising, the water has to reach the shoulders. Both hands are touching the bottom of the pool, shifting forward or back with the body position, or the arms are elevated for balance due to the action of the exercise. Keep stomach muscles tight. All of these sitting exercises can be done in deep water using the hands for sculling or finning.

Description: ## Position, Body benefit:

193. *Alternating knee lift*

Sitting upright, with hands
down, lift knee until foot is
flat on floor, alternate left
and right.   Stomach
muscles are tight.

Stomach

194. *Double knee lift*

Sitting upright, with hands
down, lift both knees until
feet are flat on floor. Extend both legs until
straight.

Stomach, back

195. *Sitting Tuck*

Feet and legs lift and extend forward. Upper torso
leans back as legs extend.

Stomach, back

196. *Straddle/press*

Sitting upright, hands are down, with legs straight forward. Press legs (apart/together) short or long straddles.

Stomach, back

197. *Cross over*

Sitting upright, hands are down. Cross legs over, left/right, left/right.

Stomach, back

198. *Simu circles*

Sitting upright, hands are down, legs are separated and forward. Simultaneous small circles forward or to each side.

Stomach, back

199. *Big wheel*

Sitting upright, hands are down. Legs are together and forward. Make big circles forward, or right/left, left/right. Can be done in deep water, legs same. Hands do sculling movements.

Stomach, back

200. *Elementaries*

Sitting upright, hands are down. Both knees are up and together, feet separated. Draw simultaneous small circles in/out, in/out.

Stomach

201. *Knee flops*

Sitting upright, hands are down. Keep knees up, toes together, down flop knees, in/out.

Stomach, thighs

202. *Scoop*

Sitting upright, hands are down. With legs together, point toes, draw knees back, push forward. Scoop water away with feet.

Stomach, back

203. *Rock the cradle*

Sitting upright, fingertips are down. Body is elevated between fingers. With legs together, straight forward, lift hips and legs far forward. Swing body down and back between arms. Legs remain straight and together.

Stomach, back

204. *Elbow to knee*

Sitting upright, bend left knee, right elbow touches left knee. Bend right knee, left elbow touches right knee, alternate.

Stomach, back

205. *Bend/extend*

Sitting upright, bend left knee, extend right arm forward. Bend right knee, extend left arm forward, alternate.

Stomach, back

206. *Row the boat*

Sitting upright, bend knees. Extend both arms far forward. Extend both legs, draw both elbows far back.

Stomach, back

Sitting Exercises with Body Elevated

While sitting in shallow water, an additional group of exercises can be performed with the body and legs in a floating position. Both hands have to be on the bottom of the pool, fingers pointing forward, with heel of hands back. The water level has to reach the shoulders, and the head should be in an upright position. Lift hips and legs and extend the body forward. Only the hands should be in contact with the pool bottom. Stomach should be tight.

Description:

Position, body benefit:

207. *Alternate knee lift*

> Backfloat position, hands are down. Lift up right knee, extend left leg forward, alternate.

Stomach

208. *Bicycle*

> Backfloat position, hands are down. Bicycle kicks forward.

Stomach

209. *Bend/extend*

> Backfloat position, hands are down. Both legs are drawn back, extended forward.

Stomach

210. *Flutters*

Backfloat position, hands are down. Both legs are extended forward, short up/down kicks. Leg movement from the hips down.

Stomach, legs

211. *Alternate scoop*

Backfloat position, hands are down. With both legs extended, point toes, alternate away kick. Scoop water on single forward kick.

Stomach, legs

212. *Double scoop*

Backfloat position, hands are down. With both legs extended, point toes, both knees bent. Scoop water on double forward kick.

Stomach, legs

213. *Crossing over*

Backfloat position, hands are down. With both legs extended, cross legs, right/left, left/right. Short or long crossings.

Stomach, hips

214. *Power press*

Backfloat position, hands are down. Legs are extended, straight, flex feet (toes up, heel down). Short or long straddle (separate legs), press together powerfully.

Stomach, back

215. *Simu loops*

Backfloat position, hands are down. With legs separated and straight, draw simultaneous loops with legs.

Stomach, back

216. *Double loop*

Backfloat position, hands are down. With legs together, bend knees, draw loop to near leg extension, right/ left, left/ right.

Stomach, legs

217. *Can-can*

Backfloat position, hands are down. Lift one leg out of the water, other leg extended in the water, alternate. This can be combined with a kick out of the water.

Stomach, legs

218. *Waist buster*

Backfloat position, hands are down.   Bend both knees, turn by waist, drop both knees to right side, raise knees, drop both knees to left side.   Knees stay pressed together.

Stomach, waist

219. *Bend 'n scoop*

Point toes, scoop water as soon as knees go into the drop position. Turn left/ right, right/left.

Stomach, waist

220. *Power knee flops*

Backfloat position, hands are down.   With feet to-gether, bend knees, pow-erfully open, press knees.

Stomach, thighs

Laying Sideways in Shallow Water

People with back problems may find the following exercises easier to tolerate in a sideways position rather than sitting with the body elevated. While in a laying position, the water should reach over the shoulders. The head should be tilted to the water side, but not submerged. The lower arm may be extended straight forward with the palms down, while the upper arm will be bent and the fingertips may touch the pool bottom in front or behind the body, depending on the exercise and balance needed.

Description: **Position, body benefit:**

221. *Alternate knee tuck*

Lay sideways with body
fully extended. Draw right
knee far toward chest, left
leg straight. Draw left knee
far toward chest, right leg
straight. Upper arm is in
front.

Stomach, back

222. *Under the bridge*

Lay sideways, body is fully
extended. Bend upper leg,
foot toward front. Straight
lower leg is under the
bridge lifting and lower-
ing. Switch sides, upper
arm in front.

Stomach, back

223. *Clap-clap*

Lay sideways, body is fully extended, straight legs. Lift slightly, separate (up/down) clap together, switch sides, upper arm in front.

Stomach, back

224. *Single leg lift*

Lay sideways, body is fully extended, lower leg slightly bent. Upper leg lifts out of the water as far as body allows. Upper arm is in front, switch sides.

Stomach, back

225. *Double leg lift*

Lay sideways, body is fully extended, both legs straight. Lift both legs slightly out of the water, with upper arm behind body, switch sides.

Stomach, back

226. *Stride step*

Lay sideways, body is fully extended, straight legs. Separate legs, one to front, one to rear. Step forward and back. Upper arm switches from front to back with balance, switch sides.

Stomach, back

227. *Kick/extend*

Lay sideways, body is fully extended, lower leg straight. Upper leg bent, drawn to chest, kick up to extend. Upper arm is in front, switch sides.

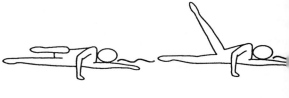

Inner thighs

228. *Double kick*

Lay sideways, both knees are bent, drawn to chest. Kick both legs forward in front of body. Upper arm behind the back, switch sides.

Stomach, back

Exercises Done Squatting, Kneeling, Laying Down

While squatting, kneeling or laying on the stomach, both hands have to be flat on the bottom of the pool, and the water should reach the shoulders in this position. In the squatting and kneeling position, we are facing several complications. Toes and knees are close to the bottom of the pool, and skin scrapes could occur while moving the legs forward and back. Knees might be bruised while in a kneeling position. Forward and back leg movements should be executed with caution. Kneeling exercises may be easier with a towel under both knees. Caution: arching of the back may cause back discomfort.

Description: **Position, body benefit:**

229. *Mountain climber*

Both hands are down, head up. One leg extends back, other leg bends forward. Hop and switch leg positions.

Thighs, stamina

230. *Squat/lift*

Both hands are down, head up. One leg bends forward, other leg extends back and up. Arch back, count 3-5 lift ups before switching legs.

Thighs, hips

231. *Squat/hop*

Both hands are down, head up. Both knees bend forward, hop to extend both legs far back. Hop forward to squatting position.

Thighs, waist

232. *Push up*

Both hands are down, head up. Both legs extend back. Bend and straighten both arms while maintaining a straight body line.

Stomach, back

233. *Hamstring*

Both hands are down, head forward. Both legs extend back. Press heel of one foot flat down, other foot lifts up to toes. Alternate heel/toe position.

Hamstring

234. *Fire hydrant*

Both hands and knees are down, head forward. Lift outer knee up (hip high), with foot same height. Lower up and down in one line, switch sides.

Thighs, hips

235. *Hydrant/extend*

See #234. After the fire hydrant lift, extend the leg out to the side and lower it, switch sides.

Thighs, hips

236. *Side bend/extend*

Hands and knees are down, head forward. Draw outer knee to chest, extend. Switch sides.

Thighs, hips

237. *Lay down kickers*

Lay on stomach, both arms extend forward, head up. Both legs are straight back.

1. Lift straight leg, left/right, right/left.

Abdomen

2. Alternating knee bends.

Upper thighs

9

Sitting on Deck

Another wonderful way to exercise the leg, stomach and back muscles is from the side of the pool, sitting on deck. Sit close to the edge of the pool and lower the legs into the water.

The following exercises can be performed in pools with the water level reaching the edge of the pool or close to it. If the thighs and abdomen are to be exercised, the body may be placed in a comfortable sitting position. Both legs should be in the water from the knees down and both hands are placed behind the body for balance.

If the thighs, abdomen and entire upper torso are to benefit, then the seat should be moved over the edge. Both legs should be straight down in the water with the upper torso leaning back slightly and both hands on the edge, fingers down. The body is almost in a straight line and all muscles are tight.

Description: **Position, Body benefit:**

238. *Alternate knee lift*

Legs together and down. Lift one knee close to the chest, other leg stays straight. Alternate up and down, point toes.

Stomach, back

239. *Double knee lift*

Legs are together and down. Lift both knees close to the chest, extend both legs straight down.

Stomach, back

240. *Straddle/press*

Legs are together, straight down. Straddle (separate legs) and press together with powerful leg movements.

Stomach, thighs, back

241. *Cross over*

Legs are together, straight down. Cross legs over, left/right, right/left.

Stomach, thighs, back

242. *Simu circles*

Legs are together, straight down. Separate legs and draw a circle simultaneously with both legs, in/out, out/in.

Stomach, thighs, back

243. *Big loop*

Legs are together, straight down. Point toes, draw big loop to the right, and to the left.

Stomach, thighs, back

244. *Stride step*

Legs are together, straight down, point toes. Alternate steps forward and back.

Stomach, thighs, back

245. *Pendulum*

Legs are together, straight down. Double leg swing left to right and right to left.

Stomach, thighs, back

246. *Flutters*

Legs are together, forward. Alternate fast paced up and down kicks.

Stomach, thighs, back

Hands move back for the following exercises:

247. *Alternating knee lift*

Legs are together, forward. Draw one knee close to chest, other leg stays straight. Alternate forward and back.

Stomach, thighs

248. *Double knee lift*

Legs are together, forward. Draw both knees up close to chest. Extend both legs forward.

Stomach, thighs

249. *Straddle press*

Legs are together, forward. Straddle (separate legs) press together, powerful leg movements.

Stomach, thighs, back

250. *Cross over*

Legs are together, forward. Cross legs over, left/right, right/left.

Stomach, thighs, back

251. *Simu circles*

Legs are together, forward. Separate legs and draw a circle simultaneously with both legs, in/out, out/in, downward.

Stomach, thighs, back

252. *Big wheel*

Legs are together, forward. Bend both knees, draw a big circle forward, down, back. Reverse.

Stomach, thighs, back

253. *Big loop*

Legs are together, forward. Draw a big circle from left to right, and from right to left.

Stomach, thighs, back

254. *Stride step*

Legs are together, forward. Press right leg straight down, left leg stays extended forward. Alternate.

Stomach, thighs, back

255. *Pendulum*

Legs are together, forward. Double leg swing to far right, and to far left.

Stomach, thighs, back

256. *Knee flops*

Feet are together, bend knees. Separate knees, press together powerfully, in/out.

Stomach, thighs, back

257. *Elbow/knee or bend/extend*

One leg is down, other knee is drawn up. Opposite elbow touches bent knee, switch. Can also be done free floating in deep water.

Stomach, back

10

Swimming

The very basic and oldest form of exercising in water is swimming. A great majority of people have tried to swim in their lifetime. Some are very successful with this art of exercising, and others are simply doing their best in moving forward in water without drowning.

The best way to be able to enjoy the full benefits of swimming is to learn how to swim the correct way. Every year classes are offered through various organizations. For instance, the American Red Cross, Swim America and YMCAs all over the country offer swimming classes for all different levels and ages. The ideal way to swim for physical fitness is to use different strokes and leg movements to be sure that all parts of the body are being exercised equally.

The different strokes most commonly used are:

- Front crawl
- Side stroke
- Breast stroke
- Back stroke

Front crawling and breast stroking involve arching and overextending the back and might not be good for the person with a back problem. Side stroking can be pretty strenuous to the neck if repeated for a longer period of time on the same side of the body. It might not be good for the person with a neck (or muscle) problem.

Back stroking seems to be the least stressful swimming exercise for the person with a back problem. Another form of swimming on the back is the elementary back stroke, which is even more recommended than the regular back stroke. By laying on the back and moving both arms only shoulder high for the out and down press, while performing a simultaneous leg circle/press action, the body is easily propelled forward into a glide.

The body remains in one straight line from the neck down. If the arms are not to be used or cannot be used, a simple flutter kicking action (up/down) will keep the person on the surface and propel him or her forward (unless the person has litttle or no buoyancy and sinks easily, in which case both arms and legs need to be used.)

Upon starting to swim, a heart rate count needs to be made and should be repeated at the end of the swimming period. The amount of laps to swim depends on the individual's physical condition and endurance. It is recommended to start gradually. Over a period of time increase swimming speed and time. It is a good idea to keep track of the amount of laps (pool widths) the individual swims during each swimming session.

Swimming in a waterobic program is an excellent way to interrupt the flow of water exercises. By adding this endurance-increasing exercise (swimming) the students receive a well-balanced physical fitness program.

After four to five minutes of swimming, followed by a heart rate count, the class will be glad to proceed with other types of movements once again.

Note: Be sure to swim in an area protected by a trained lifeguard.

Front Crawl

Front crawling is most always performed with rhythmic breathing, which means taking a breath after every second, third, or fourth arm stroke. This will allow the swimmer to continue with an uninterrupted flow of swimming. In order to take a breath of air, the head should be turned toward one shoulder just far enough for the mouth to clear the water precisely at the moment when the upper arm is extended far back.

As soon as the upper arm lifts to reach over the head, the

face should roll downward into the water where exhaling takes place, while the upper arm extends far forward and down and presses toward the hips under the water. The other arm performs the same movement in the opposite body direction. One arm is always reaching forward, while at the same time the other arm is pressing toward the hips below the body. The legs are moving with a continuous flutter kicking action (up and down).

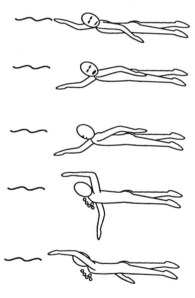

Breast stroke

The breast stroke involves a face-down body position with a rhythmical breathing action while using the arms and legs. (Some people prefer to hold the head up far enough to avoid getting the face wet.) With a forward pushing move, the hands clasp together (as in clapping) and the arms fully extend forward. As the legs straighten out behind the body, and the face is in the water, a gliding action is achieved, and the air is exhaled in the water. After the glide, hands and arms separate toward each side of the body with the palms against the water pressure, and continue to press out and down to the midsection under the body where the hands meet again for the forward extension and glide.

During this arm pressing action, the face is lifted for the mouth to clear the water, and an inhale takes place. As the arms begin to bend and separate, the legs perform a similar move. While the legs are still close together, both knees bend upward followed by a simultaneous separation of the feet, and a circle out/pressing together movement. Some people refer to this as the "frog kick."

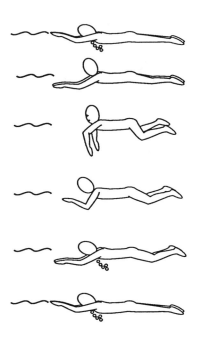

Elementary Backstroke

A person who is able to float on the back, but suffering from back problems, shoulder problems, or elbow problems might prefer the elementary backstroke.

While laying on the back, both arms simultaneously reach up on the side of the body until the hands are near the arm pits, then both arms reach far out to each side (shoulder high) to press down toward the hips with a powerful move.

At the same time as the arms reach up and out, the legs stay pressed together by the knees and bent backwards/down to continue with simultaneous leg circle/pressing action below the knees. The feet separate before the knees do. As the arms press toward the hips the legs straighten out, which will give the body a "torpedo"-like forward gliding action. Head, neck, and spine stay in a straight line during this swim stroke.

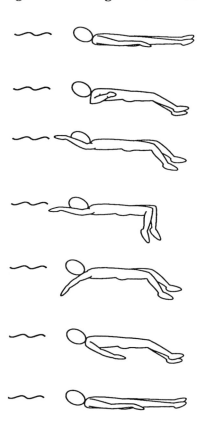

Back stroke

A person who is able to float on the back can easily learn a backstroke. The face stays out of the water the entire time while swimming, and the back stroke is much less strenuous to the cardiorespiratory system than some of the other methods of swimming.

The body may be smoothly propelled by a simultaneous up and back armstroke out of the water with one arm and a downward and side press in the water with the other arm. The leg movements are the flutter kicks (up/down).

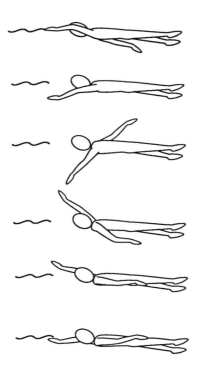

Side stroke

The side stroke involves a sideways body position with one arm fully extended beyond the head and the other arm pressing in front of the body, from the midsection down toward the upper hip.

As the arms reach and press, the legs separate far to the front, and far to the back followed by a powerful leg press together. As the arms are fully extended (one overhead, the other over the upper hip). The legs should have completed the pressing action, which at that moment gives the body a forward gliding movement.

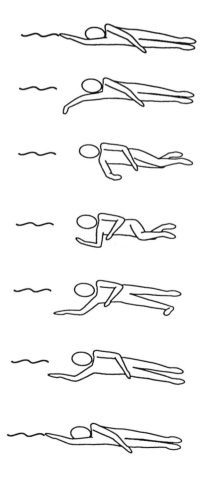

Lap Swimming

Another means of gaining or maintaining physical fitness is the uninterrupted form of swimming in a swimming pool. In aquatic terms, swimming in a pool from one side to the opposite side is called swimming one lap.

Many people substitute other activities such as running, biking, racquetball, indoor aerobics, or speed walking by swimming as many laps as they can within a certain time span. In time, speed and amount of laps will increase as the swimmer improves his physical fitness level and method of swimming. Any type of swimming may be used for lap swimming, as long as it can be done comfortably.

Upon starting lap swimming for the very first time, one should first be oriented about the width of the pool he or she is about to swim in and the equivalency per laps to miles. It is also important to be aware of the resting heart rate before starting to swim (one method of determining the heart rate is to count the heart beat for six seconds and then multiply the result times ten.)

In the beginning one may only be capable of swimming one or two uninterrupted laps. This is quite normal even if the body is used to other physical fitness methods. In swimming, until smooth forward movement has been achieved, the body and the cardiovascular system have to undergo some adjustments first. Once rhythmical breathing in coordination with arm and leg movement has been established, a smooth flow of uninterrupted swimming will become more and more possible.

In a standard size swimming pool with a width of twenty-five yards, the equivalency of laps to miles is approximately as follows:

Laps	Miles
18	1/4
36	1/2
54	3/4
72	1

However, not all swimming pools are 25 yards in width. In a pool 12 1/2 yards wide simply double the amount of laps in order to swim the equivalency of miles you want to accomplish.

Note of caution: If your usual activity is slow paced, start your exercise/swimming activity slow paced. With gradually increasing strength and stamina the tempo of your physical activity should increase. If at any time during swimming, your body or any part of your body begins to tingle, and/or you experience difficulty in breathing: stop swimming. Take your heart rate and relax. The body gives us signals when we overdo things. Let's learn to listen to the body and act accordingly.

For lap swimming as well as for other means of physical fitness activities, a word of advice should be said:

Let a doctor evaluate your present physical condition, and follow your doctor's recommendation as to what your new physical activity should be. With your doctor's approval, only you may then choose the kind of physical activity most suitable for you. Most doctors recommend in-water physical fitness activities. With all physical fitness activities it is recommended to monitor one's own heart rate at any time necessary, or regularly in each exercise period before, during, and after the entire length of physical activity.

11

Flippers

The use of flippers on the feet while performing a kicking action in the water is another great method to strengthen the legs—in particular the calf and upper thigh muscles.

The exerciser does not necessarily have to be swimming while using flippers. They can easily be used simply by sitting on the edge of a pool with the feet in the water, sitting, or even laying on the stomach in shallow or deep water. Another position might be laying sideways in shallow or deep water. Laying on the back is the most tolerable way to handle flippers on the feet.

Beginners should hold onto either a kickboard or other type of flotation equipment for balance and stability while getting used to the movement of the flippers when swimming. A steady alternating up and down kick is used with little bending of the legs for forward movement in the water, preferably using the leg

as a whole unit from the hip down. The foot remains very limber in the "shoe" portion of the flipper. The extending part of the flipper (front) will move according to the up/down leg action in a somewhat delayed move in the opposite direction of the kick. The larger the flipper and harder the kick, the greater will be the water repression. This means swimming with flippers gives faster forward propulsion. Keep the flippers as submerged as possible while using them for swimming exercises.

A note of caution: foot, leg (calf,thigh) cramps can occur easily while using the flippers.

Using the Flippers

Flippers can be used:

A.   While sitting on the edge of a pool with both legs in the water.
B.   Sitting in shallow water with both hands on the bottom of the pool and the seat raised up—for more flipper space, the entire body will have to be elevated to the water surface.

Flippers with the enclosed back are preferable to those with straps for water exercising

Flippers add additional water resistance to your workout

The flippers will become an excellent exercise tool for the stomach, back, inner and outer thigh, calf and shin muscles, as well as a strengthener for the feet. All leg movements from the exercises described in skills 206 through 212 can now be used.

The flutter kick and the dolphin kick in this position are great leg strengtheners for the person learning to use the flippers and for the person prone to leg cramps who wants to start out easy and needs to remove the flippers on first signs of muscle tenseness. If cramping occurs:

1.   Remove the flippers immediately
2.   Straighten the afflicted leg and draw the toes as far back as you can
3.   Rub/massage the afflicted area with your hands
4.   In severe cases apply pressure to the leg above the area of the cramping muscle with the heal of one hand until the muscle relaxes.

Face above the water in the prone, back, and sideways position:

A.   Beginners hold onto the side of the pool
B.   Beginners hold onto a kickboard
C.   Beginners hold onto the pull buoy
D.   Beginners place hands on bottom in shallow water

Flippers with pull buoys add greater resistance to your deep water workout

Both arms are extended straight forward, the face remains above water (unless diving) the body is fully extended: use an alternating up and down kick, originating at the hip (not at the knee) in the side position use an alternating forward and back stepping kick. Underwater/submerging: arms may be placed to each side of the body—eyes focusing forward—arms have to reach above the head upon surfacing for personal safety.

Description: **Position, Body benefit:**

248. *Prone flutter*

Alternate up and down
kick.

Thigh, calf, back

249. *Prone dolphin*

Feet together, simulta-
neous kick.

Thigh, back

250. *Side flutter*

Alternate forward and
back stepping kick. Lay-
ing sideways, one hand
holding flotation device.

Thigh, calf

251. *Side dolphin*

Feet together, simulta-
neous kick.

Thigh, stomach

252. *Back flutter*

Alternate up and down
kick. While laying on
back, both hands hold
flotation device.

A - near hips
B - over head

Thigh, calf, stomach

253. *Back dolphin*

Feet together, simulta-
neous kick

Thigh, stomach

Holding onto the edge of the pool with both hands facing
the poolside might be the most logical way to exercise with the
flippers on the feet in a vertical body position. If more distance
from the wall is needed, a simple tuck of the stomach and
bending of the back will increase the space needed for the flippers
below: stomach, back, inner and outer thighs, calves, shin muscles
and feet can thus be exercised.

254. *Vertical flutter*

Alternate forward and back kick. Body is straight, legs and abdominals tight.

Thigh, calf, stomach

255. *Vertical dolphin*

Feet together, simultaneous kick.

Thigh, stomach

256. *Toe-heel*

A - Alternate up and down foot press.

B - Simultaneous up and down foot press.

Shin

257. *Heel kick*

> A - Alternate up and down heel kick toward back. Let flipper rise and press down.

> B - Simultaneous heel kick toward back. Let flipper rise/press down.

Hamstring

258. *Sweep across*

> Bend one leg, turn knee out. Sweep flipper in front of other leg, until fully extended. Do same with other leg, opposite side.

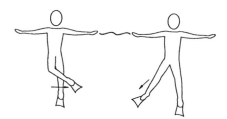

Inner thigh

259. *"Mermaid" kick*

> Legs/feet are together. Far below perform butterfly kicks (short fast movements). Use arms as for water treading.

Thigh, stomach, calf, shin

260. *Sea horse kick*

Same leg position as in 259. Kick heels as high toward back as possible, archig the back. Tilt head back, place hands at waist line, with rocking body movement, while kicking up and down.

Upper Thighs

261. *"Seal" kick*

Legs straight down, turn knees/flippers outward. Separate legs by bending knees and pushing legs apart, followed by pressing feet/flippers together as in slow motion. Clapping, use arms as in water treading. (option: hold onto pool side or flotation device).

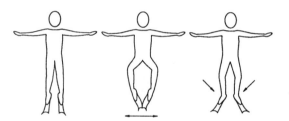

Thighs

262. *"Seal" kick*

Laying on the back- Arms may be extended overhead, floating device may be held .

Thighs

263. *"Seal" kick*

Laying sideways-
Lower arm extended
straight forward holding
flotation device, upper
arm extended toward
thigh.

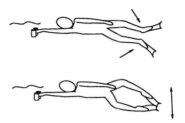

Thighs

264. *"Seal" kick*

Laying on the stomach-
Arms extended forward
holding floating device,
face may be in the water.

Thighs

Bibliography

Conrad, C. 1985. *The New Aqua Dynamics*. Alexandria, VA: National Spa and Pool Institute (NSPI).

Council on Physical Fitness. 1983. Aqua Dynamics. Washington,DC: Department of Health and Human Services.

Dominguez, R. 1980. *The Complete Book of Sports Medicine*. New York: Warner Books.

Forstreuter, H. 1974. *Koerperschule Ohne Geraet*. Frankfurt/Main, Germany: Limpert Verlap.

Good Housekeeping Editors. 1987. *Family Health and Medical Guide*. Good Housekeeping.

Kantu, R. 1983. *Exercise Injuries*. Washington, DC: Stone Wall Press.

Kos, B., Z. Teply, R. Volrab. 1973. *Gymnastik*. 1200 Uebungen, Berlin, Berman: Sportverlag.

Krasevec, J., D. Grimes. 1985. *HydroRobics*. Champaign, Illinois: Leisure Press.

Kukuk, H. U. Voncken. 1981. *111 X Wassrgymnastik Fuer Jedermann*. Schorndrf, Germany: Hofman Verlag.

Southmayd, W., M. Hoffman. 1981. *Sports Health, Complete Book of Athletic Injuries*. New York: Putnam Publishers.

Index

Treading water, 69
Tuck forward, 55
Tuck: press arms, warm up, cool down, 44

U

Under current, kickboard, 77
Under the bridge, shallow water, 104
Upper torso rotation, 54

V

Vertical dolphin, flippers, 133
Vertical flutter, flippers, 133

Another aquatic book from Sagamore Publishing:

1-2-3 Underwater Baby:
Step-by-Step Parent-Child Swim Program
Ursula Pahlow

This manual presents instructions to help teach infants and young children breath-holding and submerging techniques as a basis for an introduction to water safety. These basic swimming skills provide a natural progression into swimming lessons once the child is older. Illustrations and photographs are included to provide visual aid to the text. A VHS video is also available, which serves as an excellent companion to this guide.

One parent, whose child participated in this program, comments, *"Thanks to you and your teaching techniques, Timmy doesn't have a fear of water. I'm so glad I started him in your 'Wonder Baby' swim class when he was seven months old. He is now almost four years old and an 'Advanced Champion' swimmer."* Another parent says, *"I am very proud of Sarah's accomplishments. We did have fun. But more importantly, she has learned to hold her breath and kick to the surface, both of which could prevent her from drowning in an emergency situation."*

Ursula Pahlow is a certified American Red Cross Water Safety Instructor, and in 1986, she presented her infant swim program at the American Red Cross Annual Water Safety Conference. She is dedicated to preventing drownings by helping parents reach the goal of teaching their infants to swim.

1-2-3 Underwater Baby: A Step-by-Step Parent-Child Swim Program is a 150-page paperback book that sells for $12.95. It is an exceptional guide for parents and swimming instructors alike. The VHS video is available for $29.95. To order, or for more information call 1-800-327-5557 or write to Sagamore Publishing, Inc. at P.O. Box 673, Champaign, IL 61824-0673.